The 2023 Latest Mediterranean Diet Cookbook

1500 Days Kitchen-Tested Recipes for Getting Your Energy Up for Building the Right Diet

Aubrey Lemieux

CONTENTS

Poultry And Meats Recipes 67

Fruits, Desserts And Snacks Recipes 78

Introduction

Aubrey Lemieux has always been passionate about health, wellness, and the transformative power of a well-balanced diet. After personally experiencing the benefits of the Mediterranean lifestyle and diet, she took it upon herself to delve deeper, not only following it strictly but also studying its history, culture, and the scientific research supporting its numerous health benefits.

She started her writing process by immersing herself in the latest research on nutrition and health, focusing particularly on studies related to the Mediterranean diet. Her commitment to providing up-to-date, evidence-based information to her readers led her to collaborate with renowned nutritionists, dieticians, and food scientists, ensuring the scientific accuracy of her work.

In the development of the recipes, Lemieux sought to strike a balance between traditional Mediterranean cuisine and the changing food landscape of the 21st century. She spent months testing and perfecting each recipe, focusing on the use of fresh, locally-sourced, and seasonal ingredients, a cornerstone of the Mediterranean diet. Her dedication to authenticity and sustainability was evident in her decision to include an array of vegan, vegetarian, and gluten-free options, making the book inclusive for a wide range of dietary preferences and restrictions.

Additionally, Lemieux traveled extensively throughout the Mediterranean region, seeking inspiration from the cuisines of Spain, Italy, Greece, and the Levant. She observed local food traditions and techniques, absorbing the rich food cultures and integrating her experiences into the recipes she developed.

Finally, Lemieux understood that the integration of a diet into everyday life could be challenging for many. Therefore, she dedicated sections of her book to practical advice, tips for meal planning and preparation, as well as guidance on how to make sustainable lifestyle changes. This practical approach, combined with an array of flavorful, easy-to-follow recipes and the latest scientific evidence, makes "The 2023 Latest Mediterranean Diet Cookbook" a comprehensive guide for anyone wishing to embrace the Mediterranean diet and lifestyle.

Writing "The 2023 Latest Mediterranean Diet Cookbook" wasn't just about creating a collection of recipes for Lemieux; it was about sharing her passion for a lifestyle that she firmly believes improves both physical and mental wellbeing. She aimed to guide her readers through a culinary journey, helping them explore the flavors of the Mediterranean while also educating them about the health benefits of the diet.

What exactly is the Mediterranean Diet?

The Mediterranean diet is a way of eating that is based on the traditional foods and drinks of the countries surrounding the Mediterranean Sea. The diet is rich in fruits, vegetables, whole grains, legumes, and olive oil, and it includes moderate amounts of fish and poultry. Dairy products, like cheese and yogurt, are eaten in moderation, and there's less emphasis on red meat. The diet also includes a moderate amount of wine, typically red, usually consumed during meals.

The Mediterranean diet is not just about the food but also emphasizes physical activity, sharing meals with others, and enjoying life. Studies have found that the Mediterranean diet can reduce the risk of heart disease, protect the brain from blood vessel damage and reduce the risk of stroke and memory loss. The term 'Mediterranean diet' is now also used to refer to a simple, light and nutritious diet that is conducive to good health.

What are the combinations of Mediterranean recipes?

- This cookbook draws on the traditional foods and ingredients found in the Mediterranean diet to create endless combinations of recipes. Here are a few examples of meals, including starters, main courses and desserts, that exemplify the vibrant, healthy and delicious nature of this way of eating:

- **Appetizers/Snacks:**

- Greek Salad: A simple, refreshing mix of cucumbers, tomatoes, olives, red onions, and feta cheese, all dressed in a light olive oil and lemon vinaigrette.

- Hummus and Whole Wheat Pita: A smooth blend of chickpeas, tahini, olive oil, garlic, and lemon juice, served as a dip with hearty whole wheat pita bread.

- **Main Dishes:**

- Grilled Fish with Quinoa and Steamed Vegetables: Fresh, sustainably-sourced fish, seasoned and grilled to perfection, served with a side of cooked quinoa and a variety of colorful, steamed vegetables.

- Mediterranean-style Chicken Kebabs: Skewers of chicken, bell peppers, and onions, marinated in a flavorful mixture of olive oil, garlic, lemon, and herbs, then grilled or roasted.

- Lentil and Vegetable Stew: A hearty, warming stew made with lentils and a medley of vegetables like carrots, onions, and tomatoes, seasoned with herbs and spices.

- **Desserts:**

- Fresh Fruit Salad: A refreshing, sweet mixture of various fresh fruits, such as oranges, apples, pears, and grapes.

- Greek Yogurt with Honey and Nuts: Creamy Greek yogurt served with a drizzle of honey and a sprinkling of nuts like almonds or walnuts for a protein-rich dessert.

- **Drink:**

- Red Wine: Moderate consumption of red wine is a part of the Mediterranean diet, typically enjoyed during meals.

Remember, the Mediterranean diet is not just about the individual ingredients, but also about the overall pattern of eating – a focus on plant-based foods, lean proteins, and healthy fats, with an emphasis on enjoying meals with family and friends. The above combinations are just suggestions, and the beauty of the Mediterranean diet is that it's highly flexible and adaptable to individual preferences and needs.

The principles of the Mediterranean diet?

The principles of the Mediterranean diet go beyond just a list of foods to eat or avoid. It's a holistic approach to eating and living, emphasizing a variety of elements. Here are the main principles:

- **Eat Primarily Plant-Based Foods:** The foundation of the Mediterranean diet is a wealth of fresh fruits and vegetables, whole grains, legumes, and nuts. The diet emphasizes variety and nutrient-dense choices.

- **Focus on Healthy Fats:** Healthy fats, like those found in olive oil, avocados, and nuts, are a mainstay of the Mediterranean diet. Olive oil, in particular, is used in almost everything, from cooking to dressings for salads.

- **Choose Lean Proteins:** Fish and poultry are the main sources of protein in this diet. Red meat is eaten only sparingly, and meals are generally built around plant proteins like legumes and nuts.

- **Include Dairy in Moderation:** Low-fat or non-fat dairy products are chosen more often than full-fat versions. Cheeses and yogurts are the main sources of dairy.

- **Red Wine in Moderation:** If consumed at all, it should be moderate, and usually with meals. Women should stick to one 5-ounce serving per day, and men to two. This aspect is optional and is not recommended for everyone.

- **Regular Physical Activity:** Regular exercise is a core principle of the Mediterranean lifestyle. It can range from formal exercise routines to more informal activities like walking or gardening.

- **Shared Meals and Mindful Eating:** Food is often enjoyed in social settings, promoting a sense of community and encouraging mindful eating. Meals are seen as an opportunity to relax and enjoy good food and good company, rather than just a way to refuel.

Remember, the Mediterranean diet is a flexible eating pattern, and there's room for personalization based on your own food preferences and nutritional needs. It's a way of life rather than a strict diet, and it's recognized for both its health benefits and its sustainability.

What are the benefits of the Mediterranean diet recipes?

The benefits of the Mediterranean diet are well-documented and extend to the specific recipes associated with it. Here are some of the key benefits of following Mediterranean diet recipes:

Heart Health: Mediterranean recipes are high in heart-healthy monounsaturated fats from foods like olive oil, nuts, and seeds, and they emphasize omega-3-rich fish over red meats high in saturated fats. As a result, they can help lower bad cholesterol levels and reduce the risk of heart disease.

Weight Management: Many Mediterranean recipes are rich in fiber from whole grains, fruits, and vegetables. Fiber not only aids in digestion but also helps you feel fuller for longer, which can prevent overeating and aid in weight management.

Improved Digestive Health: The Mediterranean diet includes plenty of whole grains and legumes, fruits, and vegetables, all of which are excellent sources of dietary fiber. This aids in regular bowel movements and contributes to a healthier gut microbiome.

Blood Sugar Control: Mediterranean recipes often have a low glycemic index because they are high in fiber and low in refined carbohydrates. This means they can help control blood sugar levels, which is particularly beneficial for those with or at risk of type 2 diabetes.

Brain Health: Some research suggests that the Mediterranean diet could help protect against cognitive decline. It's thought that the combination of antioxidants and healthy fats, particularly omega-3 fatty acids found in fish, have a positive effect on brain health.

Increased Longevity: Several studies have linked the Mediterranean diet with a longer lifespan, likely due to its ability to help prevent a number of chronic diseases.

In addition to these benefits, the Mediterranean diet recipes offer a rich diversity of flavors and textures, making healthy eating both satisfying and enjoyable. It's worth noting that these benefits are more likely to be seen when the diet is followed in its entirety, as part of a balanced lifestyle that includes regular physical activity.

Breakfast Recipes

Skillet Eggplant & Kale Frittata

Servings:1
Cooking Time:20 Minutes
Ingredients:

- 1 tbsp olive oil
- 3 large eggs
- 1 tsp milk
- 1 cup curly kale, torn
- ½ eggplant, peeled and diced
- ¼ red bell pepper, chopped
- Salt and black pepper to taste
- 1 oz crumbled Goat cheese

Directions:

1. Preheat your broiler. Whisk the eggs with milk, salt, and pepper until just combined. Heat the olive oil in a small skillet over medium heat. Spread the eggs on the bottom and add the kale on top in an even layer; top with veggies.
2. Season with salt and pepper. Allow the eggs and vegetables to cook 3 to 5 minutes until the bottom half of the eggs are firm and vegetables are tender. Top with the crumbled Goat cheese and place under the broiler for 5 minutes until the eggs are firm in the middle and the cheese has melted. Slice into wedges and serve immediately.

Nutrition Info:

- Per Serving: Calories: 622;Fat: 39g;Protein: 41g;Carbs: 33g.

Classic Spanish Tortilla With Tuna

Servings:4
Cooking Time:30 Minutes
Ingredients:

- 7 oz canned tuna packed in water, flaked
- 2 plum tomatoes, seeded and diced
- 2 tbsp olive oil
- 6 large eggs, beaten
- 2 small potatoes, diced
- 2 green onions, chopped
- 1 roasted red bell pepper, sliced
- 1 tsp dried tarragon

Directions:

1. Preheat your broiler to high. Heat the olive oil in a skillet over medium heat. Fry the potatoes for 7 minutes until slightly soft. Add the green onions and cook for 3 minutes. Stir in the tuna, tomatoes, peppers, tarragon, and eggs. Cook for 8-10 minutes until the eggs are bubbling from the bottom and the bottom is slightly brown. Place the skillet under the preheated broiler for 5-6 minutes or until the middle is set and the top is slightly brown. Serve sliced into wedges.

Nutrition Info:

- Per Serving: Calories: 422;Fat: 21g;Protein: 14g;Carbs: 46g.

Creamy Peach Smoothie

Servings:2
Cooking Time: 0 Minutes
Ingredients:

- 2 cups packed frozen peaches, partially thawed
- ½ ripe avocado
- ½ cup plain or vanilla Greek yogurt
- 2 tablespoons flax meal
- 1 tablespoon honey
- 1 teaspoon orange extract
- 1 teaspoon vanilla extract

Directions:

1. Place all the ingredients in a blender and blend until completely mixed and smooth.
2. Divide the mixture into two bowls and serve immediately.

Nutrition Info:

- Per Serving: Calories: 212;Fat: 13.1g;Protein: 6.0g;Carbs: 22.5g.

Artichoke Omelet With Goat Cheese

Servings:2
Cooking Time:20 Minutes
Ingredients:

- 1 cup canned artichoke hearts, chopped
- 1 tsp butter
- 4 eggs
- Salt and black pepper to taste
- 2 small tomato, chopped
- 4 oz goat cheese, crumbled

Directions:

1. Whisk the eggs with salt and pepper in a bowl. Melt butter in a skillet over medium heat and pour in the eggs, swirling the skillet until the base is golden, 4 minutes. Add the tomato, artichoke, and goat cheese and fold over the omelet. Serve.

Nutrition Info:

- Per Serving: Calories: 310;Fat: 20g;Protein: 23g;Carbs: 16g.

Hot Zucchini & Egg Nests

Servings:4
Cooking Time:25 Minutes
Ingredients:

- 2 tbsp olive oil
- 4 eggs
- 1 lb zucchinis, shredded
- Salt and black pepper to taste
- ½ red chili pepper, minced
- 2 tbsp parsley, chopped

Directions:
1. Preheat the oven to 360 F. Combine zucchini, salt, pepper, and olive oil in a bowl. Form nest shapes with a spoon onto a greased baking sheet. Crack an egg into each nest and season with salt, pepper, and chili pepper. Bake for 11 minutes. Serve topped with parsley.

Nutrition Info:
- Per Serving: Calories: 141;Fat: 11.6g;Protein: 7g;Carbs: 4.2g.

Granola & Berry Parfait

Servings:2
Cooking Time:5 Minutes
Ingredients:

- 2 cups berries
- 1 ½ cups Greek yogurt
- 1 tbsp powdered sugar
- ¼ cup granola

Directions:
1. Divide between two bowls a layer of berries, yogurt, and powdered sugar. Scatter with granola and serve.

Nutrition Info:
- Per Serving: Calories: 244;Fat: 11g;Protein: 21g;Carbs: 43g.

Zucchini & Tomato Cheese Tart

Servings:6
Cooking Time:60 Minutes
Ingredients:

- 3 tbsp olive oil
- 5 sun-dried tomatoes, chopped
- 1 prepared pie crust
- 1 onion, chopped
- 2 garlic cloves, minced
- 2 zucchinis, chopped
- 1 red bell pepper, chopped
- 6 Kalamata olives, sliced
- 1 tsp fresh dill, chopped
- ½ cup Greek yogurt
- 1 cup feta cheese, crumbled
- 4 eggs
- 1 ½ cups milk

- Salt and black pepper to taste

Directions:
1. Preheat the oven to 380 F. Warm the olive oil in a skillet over medium heat and sauté garlic and onion for 3 minutes. Add in bell pepper and zucchini and sauté for another 3 minutes. Stir in olives, dill, salt, and pepper for 1-2 minutes and add tomatoes and feta cheese. Mix well and turn the heat off.

2. Press the crust gently into a lightly greased pie dish and prick it with a fork. Bake in the oven for 10-15 minutes until pale gold. Spread the zucchini mixture over the pie crust. Whisk the eggs with salt, pepper, milk, and yogurt in a bowl, then pour over the zucchini layer. Bake for 25-30 minutes until golden brown. Let cool before serving.

Nutrition Info:
- Per Serving: Calories: 220;Fat: 16g;Protein: 10g;Carbs: 14g.

Falafel Balls With Tahini Sauce

Servings:4
Cooking Time: 20 Minutes
Ingredients:

- Tahini Sauce:
- ½ cup tahini
- 2 tablespoons lemon juice
- ¼ cup finely chopped flat-leaf parsley
- 2 cloves garlic, minced
- ½ cup cold water, as needed
- Falafel:
- 1 cup dried chickpeas, soaked overnight, drained
- ¼ cup chopped flat-leaf parsley
- ¼ cup chopped cilantro
- 1 large onion, chopped
- 1 teaspoon cumin
- ½ teaspoon chili flakes
- 4 cloves garlic
- 1 teaspoon sea salt
- 5 tablespoons almond flour
- 1½ teaspoons baking soda, dissolved in 1 teaspoon water
- 2 cups peanut oil
- 1 medium bell pepper, chopped
- 1 medium tomato, chopped
- 4 whole-wheat pita breads

Directions:
1. Make the Tahini Sauce:
2. Combine the ingredients for the tahini sauce in a small bowl. Stir to mix well until smooth.
3. Wrap the bowl in plastic and refrigerate until ready to serve.
4. Make the Falafel:

5. Put the chickpeas, parsley, cilantro, onion, cumin, chili flakes, garlic, and salt in a food processor. Pulse to mix well but not puréed.

6. Add the flour and baking soda to the food processor, then pulse to form a smooth and tight dough.

7. Put the dough in a large bowl and wrap in plastic. Refrigerate for at least 2 hours to let it rise.

8. Divide and shape the dough into walnut-sized small balls.

9. Pour the peanut oil in a large pot and heat over high heat until the temperature of the oil reaches 375°F.

10. Drop 6 balls into the oil each time, and fry for 5 minutes or until golden brown and crispy. Turn the balls with a strainer to make them fried evenly.

11. Transfer the balls on paper towels with the strainer, then drain the oil from the balls.

12. Roast the pita breads in the oven for 5 minutes or until golden brown, if needed, then stuff the pitas with falafel balls and top with bell peppers and tomatoes. Drizzle with tahini sauce and serve immediately.

Nutrition Info:
- Per Serving: Calories: 574;Fat: 27.1g;Protein: 19.8g;Carbs: 69.7g.

Mushroom & Zucchini Egg Muffins

Servings:4
Cooking Time:20 Minutes
Ingredients:
- 2 tbsp olive oil
- 1 cup Parmesan, grated
- 1 onion, chopped
- 1 cup mushrooms, sliced
- 1 red bell pepper, chopped
- 1 zucchini, chopped
- Salt and black pepper to taste
- 8 eggs, whisked
- 2 tbsp chives, chopped

Directions:
1. Preheat the oven to 360 F. Warm the olive oil in a skillet over medium heat and sauté onion, bell pepper, zucchini, mushrooms, salt, and pepper for 5 minutes until tender. Mix with eggs and season with salt and pepper. Distribute the mixture across muffin cups and top with the Parmesan cheese. Sprinkle with chives and bake for 10 minutes. Serve.

Nutrition Info:
- Per Serving: Calories: 60;Fat: 4g;Protein: 5g;Carbs: 4g.

Spinach And Egg Breakfast Wraps

Servings:2
Cooking Time: 7 Minutes
Ingredients:
- 1 tablespoon olive oil
- ¼ cup minced onion

- 3 to 4 tablespoons minced sun-dried tomatoes in olive oil and herbs
- 3 large eggs, whisked
- 1½ cups packed baby spinach
- 1 ounce crumbled feta cheese
- Salt, to taste
- 2 whole-wheat tortillas

Directions:
1. Heat the olive oil in a large skillet over medium-high heat.

2. Sauté the onion and tomatoes for about 3 minutes, stirring occasionally, until softened.

3. Reduce the heat to medium. Add the whisked eggs and stir-fry for 1 to 2 minutes.

4. Stir in the baby spinach and scatter with the crumbled feta cheese. Season as needed with salt.

5. Remove the egg mixture from the heat to a plate. Set aside.

6. Working in batches, place 2 tortillas on a microwave-safe dish and microwave for about 20 seconds to make them warm.

7. Spoon half of the egg mixture into each tortilla. Fold them in half and roll up, then serve.

Nutrition Info:
- Per Serving: Calories: 434;Fat: 28.1g;Protein: 17.2g;Carbs: 30.8g.

Easy Zucchini & Egg Stuffed Tomatoes

Servings:4
Cooking Time:40 Minutes
Ingredients:
- 1 tbsp olive oil
- 1 small zucchini, grated
- 8 tomatoes, insides scooped
- 8 eggs
- Salt and black pepper to taste

Directions:
1. Preheat the oven to 360 F. Place tomatoes on a greased baking dish. Mix the zucchini with olive oil, salt, and pepper. Divide the mixture between the tomatoes and crack an egg on each one. Bake for 20-25 minutes. Serve warm.

Nutrition Info:
- Per Serving: Calories: 280;Fat: 22g;Protein: 14g;Carbs: 12g.

Kale-proscuitto Porridge

Servings:2
Cooking Time:30 Minutes
Ingredients:
- 1 tbsp olive oil
- 1 green onion, chopped
- 1 oz prosciutto, chopped
- 2 cups kale
- ¾ cup old-fashioned oats
- 2 tbsp Parmesan, grated
- Salt and black pepper to taste

Directions:
1. Warm the olive oil in a pan over medium heat. Sauté the onion and prosciutto and sauté for 4 minutes or until the prosciutto is crisp and the onion turns golden. Add the kale and stir for 5 minutes until wilted. Transfer to a bowl.
2. Add the oats to the pan and let them toast for 2 minutes. Add 1 ½ of water or chicken stock and bring to a boil. Reduce the heat to low, cover, and let the oats simmer for 10 minutes or until the liquid is absorbed and the oats are tender.
3. Stir in Parmesan cheese, and add the onions, prosciutto, and kale back to the pan and cook until creamy but not dry. Adjust the seasoning with salt and pepper and serve.

Nutrition Info:
- Per Serving: Calories: 258;Fat: 12g;Protein: 11g;Carbs: 29g.

Cream Peach Smoothie

Servings:1
Cooking Time:5 Minutes
Ingredients:
- 1 large peach, sliced
- 6 oz peach Greek yogurt
- 2 tbsp almond milk
- 2 ice cubes

Directions:
1. Blend the peach, yogurt, almond milk, and ice cubes in your food processor until thick and creamy. Serve and enjoy!

Nutrition Info:
- Per Serving: Calories: 228;Fat: 3g;Protein: 11g;Carbs: 41.6g.

Classic Socca

Servings:4
Cooking Time: 10 Minutes
Ingredients:
- 1½ cups chickpea flour
- ½ teaspoon ground turmeric
- ½ teaspoon sea salt
- ½ teaspoon ground black pepper
- 2 tablespoons plus 2 teaspoons extra-virgin olive oil
- 1½ cups water

Directions:

1. Combine the chickpea flour, turmeric, salt, and black pepper in a bowl. Stir to mix well, then gently mix in 2 tablespoons of olive oil and water. Stir to mix until smooth.
2. Heat 2 teaspoons of olive oil in an 8-inch nonstick skillet over medium-high heat until shimmering.
3. Add half cup of the mixture into the skillet and swirl the skillet so the mixture coat the bottom evenly.
4. Cook for 5 minutes or until lightly browned and crispy. Flip the socca halfway through the cooking time. Repeat with the remaining mixture.
5. Slice and serve warm.

Nutrition Info:
- Per Serving: Calories: 207;Fat: 10.2g;Protein: 7.9g;Carbs: 20.7g.

Raspberry-yogurt Smoothie

Servings:2
Cooking Time:10 Minutes
Ingredients:
- 2 cups raspberries
- 1 tsp honey
- 1 cup natural yogurt
- ½ cup milk
- 8 ice cubes

Directions:
1. In a food processor, combine yogurt, raspberries, honey, and milk. Blitz until smooth. Add in ice cubes and pulse until uniform. Serve right away.

Nutrition Info:
- Per Serving: Calories: 187;Fat: 7g;Protein: 8g;Carbs: 26g.

Lime Watermelon Yogurt Smoothie

Servings:6
Cooking Time:5 Minutes
Ingredients:
- ½ cup almond milk
- 2 cups watermelon, cubed
- ½ cup Greek yogurt
- ½ tsp lime zest

Directions:
1. In a food processor, blend watermelon, almond milk, lime zest, and yogurt until smooth. Serve into glasses.

Nutrition Info:
- Per Serving: Calories: 260;Fat: 10g;Protein: 2g;Carbs: 6g.

Maple Berry & Walnut Oatmeal

Servings:2
Cooking Time:10 Minutes
Ingredients:

- 1 cup mixed berries
- 1 ½ cups rolled oats
- 2 tbsp walnuts, chopped
- 2 tsp maple syrup

Directions:

1. Cook the oats according to the package instructions and share in 2 bowls. Microwave the maple syrup and berries for 30 seconds; stir well. Pour over each bowl. Top with walnuts.

Nutrition Info:

- Per Serving: Calories: 262;Fat: 10g;Protein: 15g;Carbs: 57g.

Tuna And Olive Salad Sandwiches

Servings:4
Cooking Time: 0 Minutes
Ingredients:

- 3 tablespoons freshly squeezed lemon juice
- 2 tablespoons extra-virgin olive oil
- 1 garlic clove, minced
- ½ teaspoon freshly ground black pepper
- 2 cans tuna, drained
- 1 can sliced olives, any green or black variety
- ½ cup chopped fresh fennel, including fronds
- 8 slices whole-grain crusty bread

Directions:

1. In a medium bowl, whisk together the lemon juice, oil, garlic, and pepper. Add the tuna, olives and fennel to the bowl. Using a fork, separate the tuna into chunks and stir to incorporate all the ingredients.
2. Divide the tuna salad equally among 4 slices of bread. Top each with the remaining bread slices.
3. Let the sandwiches sit for at least 5 minutes so the zesty filling can soak into the bread before serving.

Nutrition Info:

- Per Serving: Calories: 952;Fat: 17.0g;Protein: 165.0g;Carbs: 37.0g.

Easy Alfalfa Sprout And Nut Rolls

Servings:16
Cooking Time: 0 Minutes
Ingredients:

- 1 cup alfalfa sprouts
- 2 tablespoons Brazil nuts
- ½ cup chopped fresh cilantro
- 2 tablespoons flaked coconut
- 1 garlic clove, minced
- 2 tablespoons ground flaxseeds
- Zest and juice of 1 lemon

- Pinch cayenne pepper
- Sea salt and freshly ground black pepper, to taste
- 1 tablespoon melted coconut oil
- 2 tablespoons water
- 2 whole-grain wraps

Directions:

1. Combine all ingredients, except for the wraps, in a food processor, then pulse to combine well until smooth.
2. Unfold the wraps on a clean work surface, then spread the mixture over the wraps. Roll the wraps up and refrigerate for 30 minutes until set.
3. Remove the rolls from the refrigerator and slice into 16 bite-sized pieces, if desired, and serve.

Nutrition Info:

- Per Serving: Calories: 67;Fat: 7.1g;Protein: 2.2g;Carbs: 2.9g.

Basic Tortilla De Patatas

Servings:4
Cooking Time:35 Minutes
Ingredients:

- 1 ½ lb gold potatoes, peeled and sliced
- ½ cup olive oil
- 1 sweet onion, thinly sliced
- 8 eggs
- ½ dried oregano
- Salt to taste

Directions:

1. Heat the olive oil in a skillet over medium heat. Fry the potatoes for 8-10 minutes, stirring often. Add in onion, oregano, and salt and cook for 5-6 minutes until the potatoes are tender and slightly golden; set aside.
2. In a bowl, beat the eggs with a pinch of salt. Add in the potato mixture and mix well. Pour into the skillet and cook for about 10-12 minutes. Flip the tortilla using a plate, and cook for 2 more minutes until nice and crispy. Slice and serve.

Nutrition Info:

- Per Serving: Calories: 440;Fat: 34g;Protein: 14g;Carbs: 22g.

Honey & Feta Frozen Yogurt

Servings:4
Cooking Time:5 Minutes + Freezing Time
Ingredients:

- 1 tbsp honey
- 1 cup Greek yogurt
- ½ cup feta cheese, crumbled
- 2 tbsp mint leaves, chopped

Directions:

1. In a food processor, blend yogurt, honey, and feta cheese until smooth. Transfer to a wide dish, cover with

plastic wrap, and put in the freezer for 2 hours or until solid. When frozen, spoon into cups, sprinkle with mint, and serve.

Nutrition Info:

- Per Serving: Calories: 170;Fat: 12g;Protein: 7g;Carbs: 13g.

Citrus French Toasts

Servings:4
Cooking Time:30 Minutes
Ingredients:

- 1 tbsp butter
- 1 orange, juiced and zested
- 4 bread slices
- 1 ½ cups milk
- 2 eggs, beaten
- 1 tsp vanilla extract
- 1 tsp ground cinnamon
- 1 tbsp powdered sugar

Directions:

1. Beat milk, eggs, vanilla, orange zest, and orange juice in a bowl. Lay the bread in a rectangular baking dish in an even layer. Cover with the egg mixture and let it stand for 10 minutes, flipping once, to absorb well.
2. Melt the butter in a skillet over medium heat and fry the bread in batches until golden brown on both sides, about 6-8 minutes. Dust with powdered sugar and cinnamon. Serve.

Nutrition Info:

- Per Serving: Calories: 160;Fat: 7.3g;Protein: 6.9g;Carbs: 17g.

Sumptuous Vegetable And Cheese Lavash Pizza

Servings:4
Cooking Time: 11 Minutes
Ingredients:

- 2 lavash breads
- 2 tablespoons extra-virgin olive oil
- 10 ounces frozen spinach, thawed and squeezed dry
- 1 cup shredded fontina cheese
- 1 tomato, cored and cut into ½-inch pieces
- ½ cup pitted large green olives, chopped
- ¼ teaspoon red pepper flakes
- 3 garlic cloves, minced
- ¼ teaspoon sea salt
- ¼ teaspoon ground black pepper
- ½ cup grated Parmesan cheese

Directions:

1. Preheat oven to 475ºF.
2. Brush the lavash breads with olive oil, then place them on two baking sheet. Heat in the preheated oven for 4 minutes or until lightly browned. Flip the breads halfway through the cooking time.

3. Meanwhile, combine the spinach, fontina cheese, tomato pieces, olives, red pepper flakes, garlic, salt, and black pepper in a large bowl. Stir to mix well.
4. Remove the lavash bread from the oven and sit them on two large plates, spread them with the spinach mixture, then scatter with the Parmesan cheese on top.
5. Bake in the oven for 7 minutes or until the cheese melts and well browned.
6. Slice and serve warm.

Nutrition Info:

- Per Serving: Calories: 431;Fat: 21.5g;Protein: 20.0g;Carbs: 38.4g.

Chili & Cheese Frittata

Servings:6
Cooking Time:35 Minutes
Ingredients:

- 2 tbsp olive oil
- 12 fresh eggs
- ¼ cup half-and-half
- Salt and black pepper to taste
- ½ chili pepper, minced
- 2 ½ cups shredded mozzarella

Directions:

1. Preheat oven to 350 F. Whisk the eggs in a bowl. Add the half-and-half, salt, and black and stir to combine. Warm the olive oil in a skillet over medium heat. Sauté the chili pepper for 2-3 minutes. Sprinkle evenly with mozzarella cheese. Pour eggs over cheese in the skillet. Place the skillet in the oven and bake for 20–25 minutes until just firm. Let cool the frittata for a few minutes and cut into wedges. Serve hot.

Nutrition Info:

- Per Serving: Calories: 381;Fat: 31g;Protein: 25g;Carbs: 2g.

Samosas In Potatoes

Servings:8
Cooking Time: 30 Minutes
Ingredients:

- 4 small potatoes
- 1 teaspoon coconut oil
- 1 small onion, finely chopped
- 1 small piece ginger, minced
- 2 garlic cloves, minced
- 2 to 3 teaspoons curry powder
- Sea salt and freshly ground black pepper, to taste
- ¼ cup frozen peas, thawed
- 2 carrots, grated
- ¼ cup chopped fresh cilantro

Directions:

1. Preheat the oven to 350ºF.

2. Poke small holes into potatoes with a fork, then wrap with aluminum foil.

3. Bake in the preheated oven for 30 minutes until tender.

4. Meanwhile, heat the coconut oil in a nonstick skillet over medium-high heat until melted.

5. Add the onion and sauté for 5 minutes or until translucent.

6. Add the ginger and garlic to the skillet and sauté for 3 minutes or until fragrant.

7. Add the curry power, salt, and ground black pepper, then stir to coat the onion. Remove them from the heat.

8. When the cooking of potatoes is complete, remove the potatoes from the foil and slice in half.

9. Hollow to potato halves with a spoon, then combine the potato fresh with sautéed onion, peas, carrots, and cilantro in a large bowl. Stir to mix well.

10. Spoon the mixture back to the tomato skins and serve immediately.

Nutrition Info:
- Per Serving: Calories: 131;Fat: 13.9g;Protein: 3.2g;Carbs: 8.8g.

Anchovy & Spinach Sandwiches

Servings:2
Cooking Time:5 Minutes
Ingredients:
- 1 avocado, mashed
- 4 anchovies, drained
- 4 whole-wheat bread slices
- 1 cup baby spinach
- 1 tomato, sliced

Directions:
1. Spread the slices of bread with avocado mash and arrange the anchovies over. Top with baby spinach and tomato slices.

Nutrition Info:
- Per Serving: Calories: 300;Fat: 12g;Protein: 5g;Carbs: 10g.

5-ingredient Quinoa Breakfast Bowls

Servings:1
Cooking Time: 17 Minutes
Ingredients:
- ¼ cup quinoa, rinsed
- ¾ cup water, plus additional as needed
- 1 carrot, grated
- ½ small broccoli head, finely chopped
- ¼ teaspoon salt
- 1 tablespoon chopped fresh dill

Directions:
1. Add the quinoa and water to a small pot over high heat and bring to a boil.

2. Once boiling, reduce the heat to low. Cover and cook for 5 minutes, stirring occasionally.

3. Stir in the carrot, broccoli, and salt and continue cooking for 1o to 12 minutes, or until the quinoa is cooked though and the vegetables are fork-tender. If the mixture gets too thick, you can add additional water as needed.

4. Add the dill and serve warm.

Nutrition Info:
- Per Serving: Calories: 219;Fat: 2.9g;Protein: 10.0g;Carbs: 40.8g.

Ham, Bean & Sweet Potato Frittata

Servings:4
Cooking Time:25 Minutes
Ingredients:
- 2 sweet potatoes, boiled and chopped
- 2 tbsp olive oil
- 4 eggs, whisked
- 1 red onion, chopped
- ¾ cup ham, chopped
- ½ cup white beans, cooked
- 2 tbsp Greek yogurt
- Salt and black pepper to taste
- 10 cherry tomatoes, halved
- ¾ cup cheddar cheese, grated

Directions:
1. Warm the olive oil in a skillet over medium heat and sauté onion for 2 minutes. Stir in sweet potatoes, ham, beans, yogurt, salt, pepper, and tomatoes and cook for another 3 minutes. Pour in eggs and cheese, lock the lid and cook for an additional 10 minutes. Cut before serving.

Nutrition Info:
- Per Serving: Calories: 280;Fat: 18g;Protein: 12g;Carbs: 9g.

Vegetable Polenta With Fried Eggs

Servings:4
Cooking Time:35 Minutes
Ingredients:
- 2 tbsp butter
- ½ tsp sea salt
- 1 cup polenta
- 4 eggs
- 2 spring onions, chopped
- 1 bell pepper, chopped
- 1 zucchini, chopped
- 1 tsp ginger-garlic paste
- 1 ½ cups vegetable broth
- ¼ tsp chili flakes, crushed
- 2 tbsp basil leaves, chopped

Directions:
1. Melt 1 tbsp of the butter in a skillet over medium heat. Place in spring onions, ginger-garlic paste, bell pepper, and zucchini and sauté for 5 minutes; set aside.

2. Pour the broth and 1 ½ cups of water in a pot and bring to a boil. Gradually whisk in polenta to avoid chunks, lower the heat, and simmer for 4-5 minutes. Keep whisking until it begins to thicken. Cook covered for 20 minutes, stirring often. Add the zucchini mixture, chili flakes, and salt and stir.

3. Heat the remaining butter in a skillet. Break the eggs and fry them until set and well cooked. Divide the polenta between bowls, top with fried eggs and basil, and serve.

Nutrition Info:
- Per Serving: Calories: 295;Fat: 12g;Protein: 11g;Carbs: 36g.

Baked Parmesan Chicken Wraps

Servings:6
Cooking Time: 18 Minutes
Ingredients:
- 1 pound boneless, skinless chicken breasts
- 1 large egg
- ¼ cup unsweetened almond milk
- ⅔ cup whole-wheat bread crumbs
- ½ cup grated Parmesan cheese
- ¾ teaspoon garlic powder, divided
- 1 cup canned low-sodium or no-salt-added crushed tomatoes
- 1 teaspoon dried oregano
- 6 whole-wheat tortillas, or whole-grain spinach wraps
- 1 cup fresh Mozzarella cheese, sliced
- 1½ cups loosely packed fresh flat-leaf (Italian) parsley, chopped
- Cooking spray

Directions:
1. Preheat the oven to 425ºF. Line a large, rimmed baking sheet with aluminum foil. Place a wire rack on the aluminum foil, and spritz the rack with nonstick cooking spray. Set aside.

2. Place the chicken breasts into a large plastic bag. With a rolling pin, pound the chicken so it is evenly flattened, about ¼ inch thick. Slice the chicken into six portions.

3. In a bowl, whisk together the egg and milk. In another bowl, stir together the bread crumbs, Parmesan cheese and ½ teaspoon of the garlic powder.

4. Dredge each chicken breast portion into the egg mixture, and then into the Parmesan crumb mixture, pressing the crumbs into the chicken so they stick. Arrange the chicken on the prepared wire rack.

5. Bake in the preheated oven for 15 to 18 minutes, or until the internal temperature of the chicken reads 165ºF on a meat thermometer and any juices run clear.

6. Transfer the chicken to a cutting board, and cut each portion diagonally into ½-inch pieces.

7. In a small, microwave-safe bowl, stir together the tomatoes, oregano, and the remaining ¼ teaspoon of the garlic powder. Cover the bowl with a paper towel and microwave for about 1 minute on high, until very hot. Set aside.

8. Wrap the tortillas in a damp paper towel and microwave for 30 to 45 seconds on high, or until warmed through.

9. Assemble the wraps: Divide the chicken slices evenly among the six tortillas and top with the sliced Mozzarella cheese. Spread 1 tablespoon of the warm tomato sauce over the cheese on each tortilla, and top each with about ¼ cup of the parsley.

10. Wrap the tortilla: Fold up the bottom of the tortilla, then fold one side over and fold the other side over the top.

11. Serve the wraps warm with the remaining sauce for dipping.

Nutrition Info:
- Per Serving: Calories: 358;Fat: 12.0g;Protein: 21.0g;Carbs: 41.0g.

Crustless Tiropita (greek Cheese Pie)

Servings:6
Cooking Time: 35 To 40 Minutes
Ingredients:
- 4 tablespoons extra-virgin olive oil, divided
- ½ cup whole-milk ricotta cheese
- 1¼ cups crumbled feta cheese
- 1 tablespoon chopped fresh dill
- 2 tablespoons chopped fresh mint
- ½ teaspoon lemon zest
- ¼ teaspoon freshly ground black pepper
- 2 large eggs
- ½ teaspoon baking powder

Directions:
1. Preheat the oven to 350ºF. Coat the bottom and sides of a baking dish with 2 tablespoons of olive oil. Set aside.

2. Mix together the ricotta and feta cheese in a medium bowl and stir with a fork until well combined. Add the dill, mint, lemon zest, and black pepper and mix well.

3. In a separate bowl, whisk together the eggs and baking powder. Pour the whisked eggs into the bowl of cheese mixture. Blend well.

4. Slowly pour the mixture into the coated baking dish and drizzle with the remaining 2 tablespoons of olive oil.

5. Bake in the preheated oven for about 35 to 40 minutes, or until the pie is browned around the edges and cooked through.

6. Cool for 5 minutes before slicing into wedges.

Nutrition Info:
- Per Serving: Calories: 181;Fat: 16.6g;Protein: 7.0g;Carbs: 1.8g.

Tuna And Hummus Wraps

Servings:2
Cooking Time: 0 Minutes
Ingredients:

* Hummus:
* 1 cup from 1 can low-sodium chickpeas, drained and rinsed
* 2 tablespoons tahini
* 1 tablespoon extra-virgin olive oil
* 1 garlic clove
* Juice of ½ lemon
* ¼ teaspoon salt
* 2 tablespoons water
* Wraps:
* 4 large lettuce leaves
* 1 can chunk light tuna packed in water, drained
* 1 red bell pepper, seeded and cut into strips
* 1 cucumber, sliced

Directions:

1. Make the Hummus
2. In a blender jar, combine the chickpeas, tahini, olive oil, garlic, lemon juice, salt, and water. Process until smooth. Taste and adjust with additional lemon juice or salt, as needed.
3. Make the Wraps
4. On each lettuce leaf, spread 1 tablespoon of hummus, and divide the tuna among the leaves. Top each with several strips of red pepper and cucumber slices.
5. Roll up the lettuce leaves, folding in the two shorter sides and rolling away from you, like a burrito. Serve immediately.

Nutrition Info:

* Per Serving: Calories: 192;Fat: 5.1g;Protein: 26.1g;Carbs: 15.1g.

Fluffy Almond Flour Pancakes With Strawberries

Servings:4
Cooking Time: 15 Minutes
Ingredients:

* 1 cup plus 2 tablespoons unsweetened almond milk
* 1 cup almond flour
* 2 large eggs, whisked
* ⅓ cup honey
* 1 teaspoon baking soda
* ¼ teaspoon salt
* 2 tablespoons extra-virgin olive oil
* 1 cup sliced strawberries

Directions:

1. Combine the almond milk, almond flour, whisked eggs, honey, baking soda, and salt in a large bowl and whisk to incorporate.

2. Heat the olive oil in a large skillet over medium-high heat.
3. Make the pancakes: Pour ⅓ cup of batter into the hot skillet and swirl the pan so the batter covers the bottom evenly. Cook for 2 to 3 minutes until the pancake turns golden brown around the edges. Gently flip the pancake with a spatula and cook for 2 to 3 minutes until cooked through. Repeat with the remaining batter.
4. Serve the pancakes with the sliced strawberries on top.

Nutrition Info:

* Per Serving: Calories: 298;Fat: 11.7g;Protein: 11.8g;Carbs: 34.8g.

Grilled Caesar Salad Sandwiches

Servings:2
Cooking Time: 5 Minutes
Ingredients:

* ¾ cup olive oil, divided
* 2 romaine lettuce hearts, left intact
* 3 to 4 anchovy fillets
* Juice of 1 lemon
* 2 to 3 cloves garlic, peeled
* 1 teaspoon Dijon mustard
* ¼ teaspoon Worcestershire sauce
* Sea salt and freshly ground pepper, to taste
* 2 slices whole-wheat bread, toasted
* Freshly grated Parmesan cheese, for serving

Directions:

1. Preheat the grill to medium-high heat and oil the grates.
2. On a cutting board, drizzle the lettuce with 1 to 2 tablespoons of olive oil and place on the grates.
3. Grill for 5 minutes, turning until lettuce is slightly charred on all sides. Let lettuce cool enough to handle.
4. In a food processor, combine the remaining olive oil with the anchovies, lemon juice, garlic, mustard, and Worcestershire sauce.
5. Pulse the ingredients until you have a smooth emulsion. Season with sea salt and freshly ground pepper to taste. Chop the lettuce in half and place on the bread.
6. Drizzle with the dressing and serve with a sprinkle of Parmesan cheese.

Nutrition Info:

* Per Serving: Calories: 949;Fat: 85.6g;Protein: 12.9g;Carbs: 34.1g.

Morning Pizza Frittata

Servings:4
Cooking Time:20 Minutes
Ingredients:

* 2 tbsp butter
* 8 oz pancetta, chopped
* ½ onion, finely chopped
* 1 cup mushrooms, sliced

- 8 large eggs, beaten
- ¼ cup heavy cream
- 1 tsp dried oregano
- ¼ tsp red pepper flakes
- ½ cup mozzarella, shredded
- 8 cherry tomatoes, halved
- 4 black olives, sliced

Directions:

1. Melt the butter in a large skillet over medium heat until. Add the pancetta and cook for 4 minutes until browned. Stir in the onion and mushrooms and cook for 3 more minutes, stirring occasionally, until the veggies are tender. In a bowl, beat the eggs, heavy cream, oregano, and red pepper flakes.

2. Pour over the veggies and pancetta. Cook for about 5-6 minutes until the eggs are set. Spread the mozzarella cheese all over and arrange the cherry tomatoes on top. Place under the preheated broiler for 4-5 minutes. Leave to cool slightly and cut into wedges. Top with sliced olives and serve warm.

Nutrition Info:

- Per Serving: Calories: 595;Fat: 43g;Protein: 38g;Carbs: 14g.

Oven-baked Mozzarella Cheese Cups

Servings:2
Cooking Time:20 Minutes

Ingredients:

- 2 eggs, whisked
- 1 tbsp chives, chopped
- 1 tbsp dill, chopped
- Salt and black pepper to taste
- 3 tbsp mozzarella, grated
- 1 tomato, chopped

Directions:

1. Preheat the oven to 400 F. Grease 2 ramekins with cooking spray. Whisk eggs, tomato, mozzarella cheese, salt, pepper, dill, and chives in a bowl. Share into each ramekin and bake for 10 minutes. Serve warm.

Nutrition Info:

- Per Serving: Calories: 110;Fat: 8g;Protein: 8g;Carbs: 3g.

Mushroom-pesto Baked Pizza

Servings:2
Cooking Time: 15 Minutes

Ingredients:

- 1 teaspoon extra-virgin olive oil
- ½ cup sliced mushrooms
- ½ red onion, sliced
- Salt and freshly ground black pepper
- ¼ cup store-bought pesto sauce
- 2 whole-wheat flatbreads
- ¼ cup shredded Mozzarella cheese

Directions:

1. Preheat the oven to 350ºF.

2. In a small skillet, heat the oil over medium heat. Add the mushrooms and onion, and season with salt and pepper. Sauté for 3 to 5 minutes until the onion and mushrooms begin to soften.

3. Spread 2 tablespoons of pesto on each flatbread.

4. Divide the mushroom-onion mixture between the two flatbreads. Top each with 2 tablespoons of cheese.

5. Place the flatbreads on a baking sheet and bake for 10 to 12 minutes until the cheese is melted and bubbly. Serve warm.

Nutrition Info:

- Per Serving: Calories: 348;Fat: 23.5g;Protein: 14.2g;Carbs: 28.1g.

Cheesy Fig Pizzas With Garlic Oil

Servings:2
Cooking Time: 10 Minutes

Ingredients:

- Dough:
- 1 cup almond flour
- 1½ cups whole-wheat flour
- ¾ teaspoon instant or rapid-rise yeast
- 2 teaspoons raw honey
- 1¼ cups ice water
- 2 tablespoons extra-virgin olive oil
- 1¾ teaspoons sea salt
- Garlic Oil:
- 4 tablespoons extra-virgin olive oil, divided
- ½ teaspoon dried thyme
- 2 garlic cloves, minced
- ⅛ teaspoon sea salt
- ½ teaspoon freshly ground pepper
- Topping:
- 1 cup fresh basil leaves
- 1 cup crumbled feta cheese
- 8 ounces fresh figs, stemmed and quartered lengthwise
- 2 tablespoons raw honey

Directions:

1. Make the Dough:

2. Combine the flours, yeast, and honey in a food processor, pulse to combine well. Gently add water while pulsing. Let the dough sit for 10 minutes.

3. Mix the olive oil and salt in the dough and knead the dough until smooth. Wrap in plastic and refrigerate for at least 1 day.

4. Make the Garlic Oil:

5. Heat 2 tablespoons of olive oil in a nonstick skillet over medium-low heat until shimmering.

6. Add the thyme, garlic, salt, and pepper and sauté for 30 seconds or until fragrant. Set them aside until ready to use.

7. Make the pizzas:

8. Preheat the oven to 500ºF. Grease two baking sheets with 2 tablespoons of olive oil.

9. Divide the dough in half and shape into two balls. Press the balls into 13-inch rounds. Sprinkle the rounds with a tough of flour if they are sticky.

10. Top the rounds with the garlic oil and basil leaves, then arrange the rounds on the baking sheets. Scatter with feta cheese and figs.

11. Put the sheets in the preheated oven and bake for 9 minutes or until lightly browned. Rotate the pizza halfway through.

12. Remove the pizzas from the oven, then discard the bay leaves. Drizzle with honey. Let sit for 5 minutes and serve immediately.

Nutrition Info:

- Per Serving: Calories: 1350;Fat: 46.5g;Protein: 27.5g;Carbs: 221.9g.

Almond Iced-coffee

Servings:1
Cooking Time:5 Minutes
Ingredients:

- 1 cup brewed black coffee, warm
- 1 tbsp olive oil
- 1 tsp MCT oil
- 1 tbsp heavy cream
- ½ tsp almond extract
- ½ tsp ground cinnamon

Directions:

1. Pour the warm coffee (not hot) into a blender. Add the olive oil, heavy cream, MCT oil, almond extract, and cinnamon. Blend well until smooth and creamy. Drink warm and enjoy.

Nutrition Info:

- Per Serving: Calories: 128;Fat: 14.2g;Protein: 0g;Carbs: 0g.

Banana & Chia Seed Oats With Walnuts

Servings:2
Cooking Time:15 Minutes
Ingredients:

- ½ cup walnuts, chopped
- 1 banana, peeled and sliced
- 1 cup Greek yogurt
- 2 dates, pitted and chopped
- 1 cup rolled oats
- 2 tbsp chia seeds

Directions:

1. Place banana, yogurt, dates, oats, and chia seeds in a bowl and blend until smooth. Let sit for 1 hour and spoon onto a bowl. Sprinkle with walnuts and serve.

Nutrition Info:

- Per Serving: Calories: 512;Fat: 24g;Protein: 25g;Carbs: 58g.

Fish And Seafood Recipes

Salmon Baked In Foil

Servings:4
Cooking Time: 25 Minutes
Ingredients:

- 2 cups cherry tomatoes
- 3 tablespoons extra-virgin olive oil
- 3 tablespoons lemon juice
- 3 tablespoons almond butter
- 1 teaspoon oregano
- ½ teaspoon salt
- 4 salmon fillets

Directions:

1. Preheat the oven to 400ºF.
2. Cut the tomatoes in half and put them in a bowl.
3. Add the olive oil, lemon juice, butter, oregano, and salt to the tomatoes and gently toss to combine.
4. Cut 4 pieces of foil, about 12-by-12 inches each.
5. Place the salmon fillets in the middle of each piece of foil.
6. Divide the tomato mixture evenly over the 4 pieces of salmon. Bring the ends of the foil together and seal to form a closed pocket.
7. Place the 4 pockets on a baking sheet. Bake in the preheated oven for 25 minutes.
8. Remove from the oven and serve on a plate.

Nutrition Info:

- Per Serving: Calories: 410;Fat: 32.0g;Protein: 30.0g;Carbs: 4.0g.

Saucy Cod With Calamari Rings

Servings:4
Cooking Time:20 Minutes
Ingredients:

- 1 lb cod, skinless and cubed
- 2 tbsp olive oil
- 1 mango, peeled and cubed
- ½ lb calamari rings
- 1 tbsp garlic chili sauce
- ¼ cup lime juice
- ½ tsp smoked paprika
- ½ tsp cumin, ground
- 2 garlic cloves, minced
- Salt and black pepper to taste

Directions:

1. Warm the olive oil in a skillet over medium heat and cook chili sauce, lime juice, paprika, cumin, garlic, salt, pepper, and mango for 3 minutes. Stir in cod and calamari and cook for another 7 minutes. Serve warm.

Nutrition Info:

- Per Serving: Calories: 290;Fat: 13g;Protein: 16g;Carbs: 12g.

Cheesy Smoked Salmon Crostini

Servings:4
Cooking Time:10 Min + Chilling Time
Ingredients:

- 4 oz smoked salmon, sliced
- 2 oz feta cheese, crumbled
- 4 oz cream cheese, softened
- 2 tbsp horseradish sauce
- 2 tsp orange zest
- 1 red onion, chopped
- 2 tbsp chives, chopped
- 1 baguette, sliced and toasted

Directions:

1. In a bowl, mix cream cheese, horseradish sauce, onion, feta cheese, and orange zest until smooth. Spread the mixture on the baguette slices. Top with salmon and chives to serve.

Nutrition Info:

- Per Serving: Calories: 290;Fat: 19g;Protein: 26g;Carbs: 5g.

Spiced Citrus Sole

Servings:4
Cooking Time: 10 Minutes
Ingredients:

- 1 teaspoon garlic powder
- 1 teaspoon chili powder
- ½ teaspoon lemon zest
- ½ teaspoon lime zest
- ¼ teaspoon smoked paprika
- ¼ teaspoon freshly ground black pepper
- Pinch sea salt
- 4 sole fillets, patted dry
- 1 tablespoon extra-virgin olive oil
- 2 teaspoons freshly squeezed lime juice

Directions:

1. Preheat the oven to 450ºF. Line a baking sheet with aluminum foil and set aside.
2. Mix together the garlic powder, chili powder, lemon zest, lime zest, paprika, pepper, and salt in a small bowl until well combined.
3. Arrange the sole fillets on the prepared baking sheet and rub the spice mixture all over the fillets until well coated. Drizzle the olive oil and lime juice over the fillets.
4. Bake in the preheated oven for about 8 minutes until flaky.
5. Remove from the heat to a plate and serve.

Nutrition Info:

- Per Serving: Calories: 183;Fat: 5.0g;Protein: 32.1g;Carbs: 0g.

Roasted Trout Stuffed With Veggies

Servings:2

Cooking Time: 25 Minutes

Ingredients:

- 2 whole trout fillets, dressed (cleaned but with bones and skin intact)
- 1 tablespoon extra-virgin olive oil
- ¼ teaspoon salt
- ⅛ teaspoon freshly ground black pepper
- 1 small onion, thinly sliced
- ½ red bell pepper, seeded and thinly sliced
- 1 poblano pepper, seeded and thinly sliced
- 2 or 3 shiitake mushrooms, sliced
- 1 lemon, sliced
- Nonstick cooking spray

Directions:

1. Preheat the oven to 425ºF. Spray a baking sheet with nonstick cooking spray.
2. Rub both trout fillets, inside and out, with the olive oil. Season with salt and pepper.
3. Mix together the onion, bell pepper, poblano pepper, and mushrooms in a large bowl. Stuff half of this mixture into the cavity of each fillet. Top the mixture with 2 or 3 lemon slices inside each fillet.
4. Place the fish on the prepared baking sheet side by side. Roast in the preheated oven for 25 minutes, or until the fish is cooked through and the vegetables are tender.
5. Remove from the oven and serve on a plate.

Nutrition Info:

- Per Serving: Calories: 453;Fat: 22.1g;Protein: 49.0g;Carbs: 13.8g.

Garlic Shrimp With Arugula Pesto

Servings:2

Cooking Time: 5 Minutes

Ingredients:

- 3 cups lightly packed arugula
- ½ cup lightly packed basil leaves
- ¼ cup walnuts
- 3 tablespoons olive oil
- 3 medium garlic cloves
- 2 tablespoons grated Parmesan cheese
- 1 tablespoon freshly squeezed lemon juice
- Salt and freshly ground black pepper, to taste
- 1 package zucchini noodles
- 8 ounces cooked, shelled shrimp
- 2 Roma tomatoes, diced

Directions:

1. Process the arugula, basil, walnuts, olive oil, garlic, Parmesan cheese, and lemon juice in a food processor until smooth, scraping down the sides as needed. Season with salt and pepper to taste.
2. Heat a skillet over medium heat. Add the pesto, zucchini noodles, and cooked shrimp. Toss to combine the sauce over the noodles and shrimp, and cook until heated through.
3. Taste and season with more salt and pepper as needed. Serve topped with the diced tomatoes.

Nutrition Info:

- Per Serving: Calories: 435;Fat: 30.2g;Protein: 33.0g;Carbs: 15.1g.

Juicy Basil-tomato Scallops

Servings:4

Cooking Time:20 Minutes

Ingredients:

- 2 tbsp olive oil
- 1 tbsp basil, chopped
- 1 lb scallops, scrubbed
- 1 tbsp garlic, minced
- 1 onion, chopped
- 6 tomatoes, cubed
- 1 cup heavy cream
- 1 tbsp parsley, chopped

Directions:

1. Warm the olive oil in a skillet over medium heat and cook garlic and onion for 2 minutes. Stir in scallops, basil, tomatoes, heavy cream, and parsley and cook for an additional 7 minutes. Serve immediately.

Nutrition Info:

- Per Serving: Calories: 270;Fat: 12g;Protein: 11g;Carbs: 17g.

Asian-inspired Tuna Lettuce Wraps

Servings:2

Cooking Time: 0 Minutes

Ingredients:

- ⅓ cup almond butter
- 1 tablespoon freshly squeezed lemon juice
- 1 teaspoon low-sodium soy sauce
- 1 teaspoon curry powder
- ½ teaspoon sriracha, or to taste
- ½ cup canned water chestnuts, drained and chopped
- 2 package tuna packed in water, drained
- 2 large butter lettuce leaves

Directions:

1. Stir together the almond butter, lemon juice, soy sauce, curry powder, sriracha in a medium bowl until well mixed. Add the water chestnuts and tuna and stir until well incorporated.

2. Place 2 butter lettuce leaves on a flat work surface, spoon half of the tuna mixture onto each leaf and roll up into a wrap. Serve immediately.

Nutrition Info:

- Per Serving: Calories: 270;Fat: 13.9g;Protein: 19.1g;Carbs: 18.5g.

Baked Halibut With Eggplants

Servings:4
Cooking Time:35 Minutes
Ingredients:

- 2 tbsp olive oil
- ¼ cup tomato sauce
- 4 halibut fillets, boneless
- 2 eggplants, sliced
- Salt and black pepper to taste
- 2 tbsp balsamic vinegar
- 2 tbsp chives, chopped

Directions:

1. Preheat the oven to 380F. Warm the olive oil in a skillet over medium heat and fry the eggplant slices for 5-6 minutes, turning once; reserve. Add the tomato sauce, salt, pepper, and vinegar to the skillet and cook for 5 minutes. Return the eggplants to the skillet and cook for 2 minutes. Remove to a plate. Place the halibut fillets on a greased baking tray and bake for 12-15 minutes. Serve the halibut over the eggplants sprinkled with chives.

Nutrition Info:

- Per Serving: Calories: 300;Fat: 13g;Protein: 16g;Carbs: 19g.

Shrimp Quinoa Bowl With Black Olives

Servings:4
Cooking Time:20 Minutes
Ingredients:

- 10 black olives, pitted and halved
- ¼ cup olive oil
- 1 cup quinoa
- 1 lemon, cut in wedges
- 1 lb shrimp, peeled and cooked
- 2 tomatoes, sliced
- 2 bell peppers, thinly sliced
- 1 red onion, chopped
- 1 tsp dried dill
- 1 tbsp fresh parsley, chopped
- Salt and black pepper to taste

Directions:

1. Place the quinoa in a pot and cover with 2 cups of water over medium heat. Bring to a boil, reduce the heat, and simmer for 12-15 minutes or until tender. Remove from heat and fluff it with a fork. Mix in the quinoa with olive oil, dill, parsley, salt, and black pepper. Stir in tomatoes, bell peppers, olives, and onion. Serve decorated with shrimp and lemon wedges.

Nutrition Info:

- Per Serving: Calories: 662;Fat: 21g;Protein: 79g;Carbs: 38g.

White Wine Cod Fillets

Servings:4
Cooking Time:40 Minutes
Ingredients:

- 4 cod fillets
- Salt and black pepper to taste
- ½ fennel seeds, ground
- 1 tbsp olive oil
- ½ cup dry white wine
- ½ cup vegetable stock
- 2 garlic cloves, minced
- 1 tsp chopped fresh sage
- 4 rosemary sprigs

Directions:

1. Preheat oven to 375 F. Season the cod fillets with salt, pepper, and ground fennel seeds and place them in a greased baking dish. Add the wine, stock, garlic, and sage and drizzle with olive oil. Cover with foil and bake for 20 minutes until the fish flakes easily with a fork. Remove the fillets from the dish. Place the liquid in a saucepan over high heat and cook, stirring frequently, until reduced by half, about 10 minutes. Serve the fish topped with sauce and fresh rosemary sprigs.

Nutrition Info:

- Per Serving: Calories: 89;Fat: 0.6g;Protein: 18g;Carbs: 1.8g.

Sicilian-style Squid With Zucchini

Servings:4
Cooking Time:25 Minutes
Ingredients:

- 2 tbsp olive oil
- 10 oz squid, cut into pieces
- 2 zucchinis, chopped
- 2 tbsp cilantro, chopped
- 1 jalapeno pepper, chopped
- 3 tbsp balsamic vinegar
- Salt and black pepper to taste
- 1 tbsp dill, chopped

Directions:

1. Warm the olive oil in a skillet over medium heat and sauté squid for 5 minutes. Stir in zucchini, cilantro, jalapeño pepper, vinegar, salt, pepper, and dill and cook for another 10 minutes. Serve right away.

Nutrition Info:

- Per Serving: Calories: 240;Fat: 16g;Protein: 12g;Carbs: 24g.

Oven-baked Spanish Salmon

Servings:4
Cooking Time:30 Minutes
Ingredients:
- 15 green pimiento-stuffed olives
- 2 small red onions, sliced
- 1 cup fennel bulbs shaved
- 1 cup cherry tomatoes
- Salt and black pepper to taste
- 1 tsp cumin seeds
- ½ tsp smoked paprika
- 4 salmon fillets
- ½ cup chicken broth
- 3 tbsp olive oil
- 2 cups cooked farro

Directions:
1. Preheat oven to 375 F. In a bowl, combine the onions, fennel, tomatoes, and olives. Season with salt, pepper, cumin, and paprika and mix well. Spread out on a greased baking dish. Arrange the fish fillets over the vegetables, season with salt, and gently pour the broth over. Drizzle with olive oil and bake for 20 minutes. Serve over farro.

Nutrition Info:
- Per Serving: Calories: 475;Fat: 18g;Protein: 50g;Carbs: 26g.

Lemon Shrimp With Black Olives

Servings:4
Cooking Time:25 Minutes
Ingredients:
- 1 lb shrimp, peeled and deveined
- 3 tbsp olive oil
- 1 lemon, juiced
- 1 tbsp flour
- 1 cup fish stock
- Salt and black pepper to taste
- 1 cup black olives, halved
- 1 tbsp rosemary, chopped

Directions:
1. Warm the olive oil in a skillet over medium heat and sear shrimp for 4 minutes on both sides; set aside. In the same skillet over low heat, stir in the flour for 2-3 minutes.
2. Gradually pour in the fish stock and lemon juice while stirring and simmer for 3-4 minutes until the sauce thickens. Adjust the seasoning with salt and pepper and mix in shrimp, olives, and rosemary. Serve immediately.

Nutrition Info:
- Per Serving: Calories: 240;Fat: 16g;Protein: 9g;Carbs: 16g.

Mediterranean Grilled Sea Bass

Servings:6
Cooking Time: 20 Minutes

Ingredients:
- ¼ teaspoon onion powder
- ¼ teaspoon garlic powder
- ¼ teaspoon paprika
- Lemon pepper and sea salt to taste
- 2 pounds sea bass
- 3 tablespoons extra-virgin olive oil, divided
- 2 large cloves garlic, chopped
- 1 tablespoon chopped Italian flat leaf parsley

Directions:
1. Preheat the grill to high heat.
2. Place the onion powder, garlic powder, paprika, lemon pepper, and sea salt in a large bowl and stir to combine.
3. Dredge the fish in the spice mixture, turning until well coated.
4. Heat 2 tablespoon of olive oil in a small skillet. Add the garlic and parsley and cook for 1 to 2 minutes, stirring occasionally. Remove the skillet from the heat and set aside.
5. Brush the grill grates lightly with remaining 1 tablespoon olive oil.
6. Grill the fish for about 7 minutes. Flip the fish and drizzle with the garlic mixture and cook for an additional 7 minutes, or until the fish flakes when pressed lightly with a fork.
7. Serve hot.

Nutrition Info:
- Per Serving: Calories: 200;Fat: 10.3g;Protein: 26.9g;Carbs: 0.6g.

Lemon-parsley Swordfish

Servings:4
Cooking Time: 17 To 20 Minutes
Ingredients:
- 1 cup fresh Italian parsley
- ¼ cup lemon juice
- ¼ cup extra-virgin olive oil
- ¼ cup fresh thyme
- 2 cloves garlic
- ½ teaspoon salt
- 4 swordfish steaks
- Olive oil spray

Directions:
1. Preheat the oven to 450ºF. Grease a large baking dish generously with olive oil spray.
2. Place the parsley, lemon juice, olive oil, thyme, garlic, and salt in a food processor and pulse until smoothly blended.
3. Arrange the swordfish steaks in the greased baking dish and spoon the parsley mixture over the top.
4. Bake in the preheated oven for 17 to 20 minutes until flaky.
5. Divide the fish among four plates and serve hot.

Nutrition Info:

- Per Serving: Calories: 396;Fat: 21.7g;Protein: 44.2g;Carbs: 2.9g.

Parsley Halibut With Roasted Peppers

Servings:4
Cooking Time:45 Minutes
Ingredients:
- 3 tbsp olive oil
- 1 tsp butter
- 2 red peppers, cut into wedges
- 4 halibut fillets
- 2 shallots, cut into rings
- 2 garlic cloves, minced
- ¾ cup breadcrumbs
- 2 tbsp chopped fresh parsley
- Salt and black pepper to taste

Directions:
1. Preheat oven to 450 F. Combine red peppers, garlic, shallots, 1 tbsp of olive oil, salt, and pepper in a bowl. Spread on a baking sheet and bake for 40 minutes. Warm the remaining olive oil in a pan over medium heat and brown the breadcrumbs for 4-5 minutes, stirring constantly. Set aside.
2. Clean the pan and add in the butter to melt. Sprinkle the fish with salt and pepper. Add to the butter and cook for 8-10 minutes on both sides. Divide the pepper mixture between 4 plates and top with halibut fillets. Spread the crunchy breadcrumbs all over and top with parsley. Serve and enjoy!

Nutrition Info:
- Per Serving: Calories: 511;Fat: 19.4g;Protein: 64g;Carbs: 18g.

Tuna And Zucchini Patties

Servings:4
Cooking Time: 12 Minutes
Ingredients:
- 3 slices whole-wheat sandwich bread, toasted
- 2 cans tuna in olive oil, drained
- 1 cup shredded zucchini
- 1 large egg, lightly beaten
- ¼ cup diced red bell pepper
- 1 tablespoon dried oregano
- 1 teaspoon lemon zest
- ¼ teaspoon freshly ground black pepper
- ¼ teaspoon kosher or sea salt
- 1 tablespoon extra-virgin olive oil
- Salad greens or 4 whole-wheat rolls, for serving (optional)

Directions:
1. Crumble the toast into bread crumbs with your fingers (or use a knife to cut into ¼-inch cubes) until you have 1 cup of loosely packed crumbs. Pour the crumbs into a large bowl. Add the tuna, zucchini, beaten egg, bell pepper, oregano, lemon zest, black pepper, and salt. Mix well with a fork. With your hands, form the mixture into four (½-cup-size) patties. Place them on a plate, and press each patty flat to about ¾-inch thick.
2. In a large skillet over medium-high heat, heat the oil until it's very hot, about 2 minutes.
3. Add the patties to the hot oil, then reduce the heat down to medium. Cook the patties for 5 minutes, flip with a spatula, and cook for an additional 5 minutes. Serve the patties on salad greens or whole-wheat rolls, if desired.

Nutrition Info:
- Per Serving: Calories: 757;Fat: 72.0g;Protein: 5.0g;Carbs: 26.0g.

Lemon Cioppino

Servings:6
Cooking Time:6 Minutes
Ingredients:
- 1 lb mussels, scrubbed, debearded
- 1 lb large shrimp, peeled and deveined
- 1 ½ lb haddock fillets, cut into chunks
- 3 tbsp olive oil
- 1 fennel bulb, thinly sliced
- 1 onion, chopped
- 3 large shallots, chopped
- Salt to taste
- 4 garlic cloves, minced
- ¼ tsp red pepper flakes
- ¼ cup tomato paste
- 1 can diced tomatoes
- 1 ½ cups dry white wine
- 5 cups vegetable stock
- 1 bay leaf
- 1 lb clams, scrubbed
- 2 tbsp basil, chopped

Directions:
1. Warm the olive oil in a large pot over medium heat. Sauté the fennel, onion, garlic, and shallots for 8-10 minutes until tender. Add the red pepper flakes and sauté for 2 minutes. Stir in the tomato paste, tomatoes with their juices, wine, stock, salt, and bay leaf. Cover and bring to a simmer. Lower the heat to low and simmer for 30 minutes until the flavors blend.
2. Pour in the clams and mussels and cook for about 5 minutes. Add the shrimp and fish. Simmer gently until the fish and shrimp are just cooked through, 5 minutes. Discard any clams and mussels that refuse to open and bay leaf. Top with basil.

Nutrition Info:
- Per Serving: Calories: 163;Fat: 4.1g;Protein: 22g;Carbs: 8.3g.

Wine-steamed Clams

Servings:4
Cooking Time:30 Minutes
Ingredients:

- 4 lb clams, scrubbed and debearded
- 3 tbsp butter
- 3 garlic cloves, minced
- ¼ tsp red pepper flakes
- 1 cup dry white wine
- 3 sprigs fresh thyme
- 2 tbsp fresh dill, minced

Directions:

1. Melt the butter in a large saucepan over medium heat and cook garlic and pepper flakes, stirring constantly, until fragrant, about 30 seconds. Stir in wine and thyme sprigs, bring to a boil and cook until wine is slightly reduced, about 1 minute. Stir in clams. Cover the saucepan and simmer for 15-18 minutes. Remove, discard thyme sprigs and any clams that refuse to open. Sprinkle with dill and serve.

Nutrition Info:

- Per Serving: Calories: 326;Fat: 14g;Protein: 36g;Carbs: 12g.

Salt And Pepper Calamari And Scallops

Servings:4
Cooking Time: 10 Minutes
Ingredients:

- 8 ounces calamari steaks, cut into ½-inch-thick rings
- 8 ounces sea scallops
- 1½ teaspoons salt, divided
- 1 teaspoon garlic powder
- 1 teaspoon freshly ground black pepper
- ⅓ cup extra-virgin olive oil
- 2 tablespoons almond butter

Directions:

1. Place the calamari and scallops on several layers of paper towels and pat dry. Sprinkle with 1 teaspoon of salt and allow to sit for 15 minutes at room temperature. Pat dry with additional paper towels. Sprinkle with pepper and garlic powder.
2. In a deep medium skillet, heat the olive oil and butter over medium-high heat. When the oil is hot but not smoking, add the scallops and calamari in a single layer to the skillet and sprinkle with the remaining ½ teaspoon of salt. Cook for 2 to 4 minutes on each side, depending on the size of the scallops, until just golden but still slightly opaque in center.
3. Using a slotted spoon, remove from the skillet and transfer to a serving platter. Allow the cooking oil to cool slightly and drizzle over the seafood before serving.

Nutrition Info:

- Per Serving: Calories: 309;Fat: 25.0g;Protein: 18.0g;Carbs: 3.0g.

Simple Salmon With Balsamic Haricots Vert

Servings:4
Cooking Time:25 Minutes
Ingredients:

- 2 tbsp olive oil
- 3 tbsp balsamic vinegar
- 1 garlic clove, minced
- ½ tsp red pepper flakes
- 1 ½ lb haricots vert, chopped
- Salt and black pepper to taste
- 1 red onion, sliced
- 4 salmon fillets, boneless

Directions:

1. Warm half of oil in a skillet over medium heat and sauté vinegar, onion, garlic, red pepper flakes, haricots vert, salt, and pepper for 6 minutes. Share into plates. Warm the remaining oil. Sprinkle salmon with salt and pepper and sear for 8 minutes on all sides. Serve with haricots vert.

Nutrition Info:

- Per Serving: Calories: 230;Fat: 16g;Protein: 17g;Carbs: 23g.

Glazed Broiled Salmon

Servings:4
Cooking Time: 5 To 10 Minutes
Ingredients:

- 4 salmon fillets
- 3 tablespoons miso paste
- 2 tablespoons raw honey
- 1 teaspoon coconut aminos
- 1 teaspoon rice vinegar

Directions:

1. Preheat the broiler to High. Line a baking dish with aluminum foil and add the salmon fillets.
2. Whisk together the miso paste, honey, coconut aminos, and vinegar in a small bowl. Pour the glaze over the fillets and spread it evenly with a brush.
3. Broil for about 5 minutes, or until the salmon is browned on top and opaque. Brush any remaining glaze over the salmon and broil for an additional 5 minutes if needed. The cooking time depends on the thickness of the salmon.
4. Let the salmon cool for 5 minutes before serving.

Nutrition Info:

- Per Serving: Calories: 263;Fat: 8.9g;Protein: 30.2g;Carbs: 12.8g.

Caper & Squid Stew

Servings:4
Cooking Time:25 Minutes
Ingredients:

- 2 tbsp olive oil
- 1 onion, chopped
- 1 celery stalk, chopped
- 1 lb calamari rings
- 2 red chili peppers, chopped
- 2 garlic cloves, minced
- 14 oz canned tomatoes, diced
- 2 tbsp tomato paste
- Salt and black pepper to taste
- 2 tbsp capers, drained
- 12 black olives, pitted and halved

Directions:
1. Warm the olive oil in a skillet over medium heat and cook onion, celery, garlic, and chili peppers for 2 minutes. Stir in calamari rings, tomatoes, tomato paste, salt, and pepper and bring to a simmer. Cook for 20 minutes. Put in olives and capers and cook for another 5 minutes. Serve right away.

Nutrition Info:
- Per Serving: Calories: 280;Fat: 12g;Protein: 16g;Carbs: 14g.

Lime-orange Squid Meal

Servings:4
Cooking Time:30 Minutes
Ingredients:

- 1 lb baby squid, cleaned, body and tentacles chopped
- 3 tbsp olive oil
- ½ cup green olives, chopped
- ½ tsp lime zest, grated
- 1 tbsp lime juice
- ½ tsp orange zest, grated
- 1 tsp red pepper flakes
- 1 tbsp parsley, chopped
- 4 garlic cloves, minced
- 1 shallot, chopped
- 1 cup vegetable stock
- 2 tbsp red wine vinegar
- Salt and black pepper to taste

Directions:
1. Warm the olive oil in a skillet over medium heat and stir in lime zest, lime juice, orange zest, red pepper flakes, garlic, shallot, olives, stock, vinegar, salt, and pepper. Bring to a boil and simmer for 10 minutes. Mix in squid and parsley and cook for another 10 minutes. Serve hot.

Nutrition Info:
- Per Serving: Calories: 310;Fat: 10g;Protein: 12g;Carbs: 23g.

Balsamic Asparagus & Salmon Roast

Servings:4
Cooking Time:20 Minutes
Ingredients:

- 2 tbsp olive oil
- 4 salmon fillets, skinless
- 2 tbsp balsamic vinegar
- 1 lb asparagus, trimmed
- Salt and black pepper to taste

Directions:
1. Preheat the oven to 380F. In a roasting pan, arrange the salmon fillets and asparagus spears. Season with salt and pepper and drizzle with olive oil and balsamic vinegar; roast for 12-15 minutes. Serve warm.

Nutrition Info:
- Per Serving: Calories: 310;Fat: 16g;Protein: 21g;Carbs: 19g.

Italian Tilapia Pilaf

Servings:2
Cooking Time:45 Minutes
Ingredients:

- 3 tbsp olive oil
- 2 tilapia fillets, boneless
- ½ tsp Italian seasoning
- ½ cup brown rice
- ½ cup green bell pepper, diced
- ½ cup white onions, chopped
- ½ tsp garlic powder
- Salt and black pepper to taste

Directions:
1. Warm 1 tbsp of olive oil in a saucepan over medium heat. Cook onions, bell pepper, garlic powder, Italian seasoning, salt, and pepper for 3 minutes. Stir in brown rice and 2 cups of water and bring to a simmer. Cook for 18 minutes. Warm the remaining oil in a skillet over medium heat. Season the tilapia with salt and pepper. Fry for 10 minutes on both sides. Share the rice among plates and top with the tilapia fillets.

Nutrition Info:
- Per Serving: Calories: 270;Fat: 18g;Protein: 13g;Carbs: 26g.

Salmon & Celery Egg Bake

Servings:4
Cooking Time:40 Minutes
Ingredients:

- 2 tbsp olive oil
- 2 tbsp butter, melted
- 4 oz smoked salmon, flaked
- 1 cup cheddar cheese, grated
- 4 eggs, whisked
- ¼ cup plain yogurt

- 1 cup cream of celery soup
- 1 shallot, chopped
- 2 garlic cloves, minced
- ½ cup celery, chopped
- 8 slices fresh toast, cubed
- 1 tbsp mint leaves, chopped

Directions:

1. Preheat the oven to 360 F. In a bowl, mix eggs, yogurt, and celery soup. Warm olive oil in a skillet over medium heat and cook the shallot, garlic, and celery until tender. Place the toast cubes in a greased baking dish, top with cooked vegetables and salmon, and cover with egg mixture and butter. Bake for 22-25 minutes until it is cooked through. Scatter cheddar cheese on top and bake for another 5 minutes until the cheese melts. Serve garnished with mint leaves.

Nutrition Info:

- Per Serving: Calories: 392;Fat: 31g;Protein: 20g;Carbs: 9.6g.

Anchovy Spread With Avocado

Servings:2
Cooking Time:5 Minutes

Ingredients:

- 1 avocado, peeled and pitted
- 1 tsp lemon juice
- ¼ celery stalk, chopped
- ¼ cup chopped shallots
- 2 anchovy fillets in olive oil
- Salt and black pepper to taste

Directions:

1. Combine lemon juice, avocado, celery, shallots, and anchovy fillets (with their olive oil) in a food processor. Blitz until smooth. Season with salt and black pepper. Serve.

Nutrition Info:

- Per Serving: Calories: 271;Fat: 20g;Protein: 15g;Carbs: 12g.

Hot Jumbo Shrimp

Servings:4
Cooking Time:20 Minutes

Ingredients:

- 2 lb shell-on jumbo shrimp, deveined
- ¼ cup olive oil
- Salt and black pepper to taste
- 6 garlic cloves, minced
- 1 tsp anise seeds
- ½ tsp red pepper flakes
- 2 tbsp minced fresh cilantro
- 1 lemon, cut into wedges

Directions:

1. Combine the olive oil, garlic, anise seeds, pepper flakes, and black pepper in a large bowl. Add the shrimp and

cilantro and toss well, making sure the oil mixture gets into the interior of the shrimp. Arrange shrimp in a single layer on a baking tray. Set under the preheated broiler for approximately 4 minutes. Flip shrimp and continue to broil until it is opaque and shells are beginning to brown, about 2 minutes, rotating sheet halfway through broiling. Serve with lemon wedges.

Nutrition Info:

- Per Serving: Calories: 218;Fat: 9g;Protein: 30.8g;Carbs: 2.3g.

Air-fried Flounder Fillets

Servings:4
Cooking Time: 12 Minutes

Ingredients:

- 2 cups unsweetened almond milk
- ½ teaspoon onion powder
- ½ teaspoon garlic powder
- 4 flounder fillets
- ½ cup chickpea flour
- ½ cup plain yellow cornmeal
- ¼ teaspoon cayenne pepper
- Freshly ground black pepper, to taste

Directions:

1. Whisk together the almond milk, onion powder, and garlic powder in a large bowl until smooth.
2. Add the flounder, coating well on both sides, and let marinate for about 20 minutes.
3. Meanwhile, combine the chickpea flour, cornmeal, cayenne, and pepper in a shallow dish.
4. Dredge each piece of flounder fillets in the flour mixture until completely coated.
5. Preheat the air fryer to 380ºF.
6. Arrange the coated flounder fillets in the basket and cook for 12 minutes, flipping them halfway through.
7. Remove from the basket and serve on a plate.

Nutrition Info:

- Per Serving: Calories: 228;Fat: 5.7g;Protein: 28.2g;Carbs: 15.5g.

Salmon And Mushroom Hash With Pesto

Servings:6
Cooking Time: 20 Minutes

Ingredients:

- Pesto:
- ¼ cup extra-virgin olive oil
- 1 bunch fresh basil
- Juice and zest of 1 lemon
- ⅓ cup water
- ¼ teaspoon salt, plus additional as needed
- Hash:
- 2 tablespoons extra-virgin olive oil

- 6 cups mixed mushrooms (brown, white, shiitake, cremini, portobello, etc.), sliced
- 1 pound wild salmon, cubed

Directions:

1.   Make the pesto: Pulse the olive oil, basil, juice and zest, water, and salt in a blender or food processor until smoothly blended. Set aside.

2.   Heat the olive oil in a large skillet over medium heat.

3.   Stir-fry the mushrooms for 6 to 8 minutes, or until they begin to exude their juices.

4.   Add the salmon and cook each side for 5 to 6 minutes until cooked through.

5.   Fold in the prepared pesto and stir well. Taste and add additional salt as needed. Serve warm.

Nutrition Info:

- Per Serving: Calories: 264;Fat: 14.7g;Protein: 7.0g;Carbs: 30.9g.

Cod Fillets In Mushroom Sauce

Servings:4
Cooking Time:45 Minutes

Ingredients:

- 2 cups cremini mushrooms, sliced
- ¼ cup olive oil
- 4 cod fillets
- ½ cup shallots, chopped
- 2 garlic cloves, minced
- 2 cups canned diced tomatoes
- ½ cup clam juice
- ¼ tsp chili flakes
- ¼ tsp sweet paprika
- 1 tbsp capers
- ¼ cup raisins, soaked
- 1 lemon, cut into wedges
- Salt to taste

Directions:

1.   Heat the oil in a skillet over medium heat. Sauté shallots and garlic for 2-3 minutes. Add in mushrooms and cook for another 4 minutes. Stir in tomatoes, clam juice, chili flakes, paprika, capers, and salt. Bring to a boil and simmer for 15 minutes.

2.   Preheat oven to 380 F. Arrange the cod fillets on a greased baking pan. Cover with the mushroom mixture and top with the soaked raisins. Bake for 18-20 minutes. Serve garnished with lemon wedges.

Nutrition Info:

- Per Serving: Calories: 317;Fat: 13g;Protein: 25g;Carbs: 26g.

Pan-fried Tuna With Vegetables

Servings:4
Cooking Time:25 Minutes
Ingredients:

- 2 tbsp olive oil
- 4 tuna fillets, boneless
- 1 red bell pepper, chopped
- 1 onion, chopped
- 4 garlic cloves, minced
- ½ cup fish stock
- 1 tsp basil, dried
- ½ cup cherry tomatoes, halved
- ½ cup black olives, halved
- Salt and black pepper to taste

Directions:

1.   Warm the olive oil in a skillet over medium heat and fry tuna for 10 minutes on both sides. Divide the fish among plates. In the same skillet, cook onion, bell pepper, garlic, and cherry tomatoes for 3 minutes. Stir in salt, pepper, fish stock, basil, and olives and cook for another 3 minutes. Top the tuna with the mixture and serve immediately.

Nutrition Info:

- Per Serving: Calories: 260;Fat: 9g;Protein: 29g;Carbs: 6g.

Easy Tomato Tuna Melts

Servings:2
Cooking Time: 3 To 4 Minutes

Ingredients:

- 1 can chunk light tuna packed in water, drained
- 2 tablespoons plain Greek yogurt
- 2 tablespoons finely chopped celery
- 1 tablespoon finely chopped red onion
- 2 teaspoons freshly squeezed lemon juice
- Pinch cayenne pepper
- 1 large tomato, cut into ¾-inch-thick rounds
- ½ cup shredded Cheddar cheese

Directions:

1.   Preheat the broiler to High.

2.   Stir together the tuna, yogurt, celery, red onion, lemon juice, and cayenne pepper in a medium bowl.

3.   Place the tomato rounds on a baking sheet. Top each with some tuna salad and Cheddar cheese.

4.   Broil for 3 to 4 minutes until the cheese is melted and bubbly. Cool for 5 minutes before serving.

Nutrition Info:

- Per Serving: Calories: 244;Fat: 10.0g;Protein: 30.1g;Carbs: 6.9g.

Parchment Orange & Dill Salmon

Servings:4
Cooking Time:25 Minutes
Ingredients:

- 2 tbsp butter, melted
- 4 salmon fillets
- Salt and black pepper to taste
- 1 orange, juiced and zested

- 4 tbsp fresh dill, chopped

Directions:

1. Preheat oven to 375 F. Coat the salmon fillets on both sides with butter. Season with salt and pepper and divide them between 4 pieces of parchment paper. Drizzle the orange juice over each piece of fish and top with orange zest and dill. Wrap the paper around the fish to make packets. Place on a baking sheet and bake for 15-20 minutes until the cod is cooked through. Serve and enjoy!

Nutrition Info:

- Per Serving: Calories: 481;Fat: 21g;Protein: 65g;Carbs: 4.2g.

Shrimp And Pea Paella

Servings:2
Cooking Time: 60 Minutes

Ingredients:

- 2 tablespoons olive oil
- 1 garlic clove, minced
- ½ large onion, minced
- 1 cup diced tomato
- ½ cup short-grain rice
- ½ teaspoon sweet paprika
- ½ cup dry white wine
- 1¼ cups low-sodium chicken stock
- 8 ounces large raw shrimp
- 1 cup frozen peas
- ¼ cup jarred roasted red peppers, cut into strips
- Salt, to taste

Directions:

1. Heat the olive oil in a large skillet over medium-high heat.
2. Add the garlic and onion and sauté for 3 minutes, or until the onion is softened.
3. Add the tomato, rice, and paprika and stir for 3 minutes to toast the rice.
4. Add the wine and chicken stock and stir to combine. Bring the mixture to a boil.
5. Cover and reduce the heat to medium-low, and simmer for 45 minutes, or until the rice is just about tender and most of the liquid has been absorbed.
6. Add the shrimp, peas, and roasted red peppers. Cover and cook for an additional 5 minutes. Season with salt to taste and serve.

Nutrition Info:

- Per Serving: Calories: 646;Fat: 27.1g;Protein: 42.0g;Carbs: 59.7g.

Classic Prawn Scampi

Servings:4
Cooking Time:25 Minutes

Ingredients:

- 1 lb prawns, peeled and deveined

- 2 tbsp olive oil
- 1 onion, chopped
- 6 garlic cloves, minced
- 1 lemon, juiced and zested
- ½ cup dry white wine
- Salt and black pepper to taste
- 2 cups fusilli, cooked
- ½ tsp red pepper flakes

Directions:

1. Warm olive oil in a pan over medium heat and sauté onion and garlic for 3 minutes, stirring often, until fragrant. Stir in prawns and cook for 3-4 minutes. Mix in lemon juice, lemon zest, salt, pepper, wine, and red flakes. Bring to a boil, then decrease the heat, and simmer for 2 minutes until the liquid is reduced by half. Turn the heat off. Stir in pasta and serve.

Nutrition Info:

- Per Serving: Calories: 388;Fat: 9g;Protein: 32g;Carbs: 38.2g.

Mediterranean Cod Stew

Servings:6
Cooking Time: 20 Minutes

Ingredients:

- 2 tablespoons extra-virgin olive oil
- 2 cups chopped onion
- 2 garlic cloves, minced
- ¾ teaspoon smoked paprika
- 1 can diced tomatoes, undrained
- 1 jar roasted red peppers, drained and chopped
- 1 cup sliced olives, green or black
- ⅓ cup dry red wine
- ¼ teaspoon kosher or sea salt
- ¼ teaspoon freshly ground black pepper
- 1½ pounds cod fillets, cut into 1-inch pieces
- 3 cups sliced mushrooms

Directions:

1. In a large stockpot over medium heat, heat the oil. Add the onion and cook for 4 minutes, stirring occasionally. Add the garlic and smoked paprika and cook for 1 minute, stirring often.
2. Mix in the tomatoes with their juices, roasted peppers, olives, wine, pepper, and salt, and turn the heat to medium-high. Bring the mixture to a boil. Add the cod fillets and mushrooms, and reduce the heat to medium.
3. Cover and cook for about 10 minutes, stirring a few times, until the cod is cooked through and flakes easily, and serve.

Nutrition Info:

- Per Serving: Calories: 167;Fat: 5.0g;Protein: 19.0g;Carbs: 11.0g.

Hazelnut Crusted Sea Bass

Servings:2
Cooking Time: 15 Minutes
Ingredients:
- 2 tablespoons almond butter
- 2 sea bass fillets
- ⅓ cup roasted hazelnuts
- A pinch of cayenne pepper

Directions:

1. Preheat the oven to 425ºF. Line a baking dish with waxed paper.
2. Brush the almond butter over the fillets.
3. Pulse the hazelnuts and cayenne in a food processor. Coat the sea bass with the hazelnut mixture, then transfer to the baking dish.
4. Bake in the preheated oven for about 15 minutes. Cool for 5 minutes before serving.

Nutrition Info:
- Per Serving: Calories: 468;Fat: 30.8g;Protein: 40.0g;Carbs: 8.8g.

Vegetable Mains And Meatless Recipes

Sweet Potato Chickpea Buddha Bowl

Servings:2
Cooking Time: 10 To 15 Minutes
Ingredients:
- Sauce:
- 1 tablespoon tahini
- 2 tablespoons plain Greek yogurt
- 2 tablespoons hemp seeds
- 1 garlic clove, minced
- Pinch salt
- Freshly ground black pepper, to taste
- Bowl:
- 1 small sweet potato, peeled and finely diced
- 1 teaspoon extra-virgin olive oil
- 1 cup from 1 can low-sodium chickpeas, drained and rinsed
- 2 cups baby kale

Directions:
1. Make the Sauce
2. Whisk together the tahini and yogurt in a small bowl.
3. Stir in the hemp seeds and minced garlic. Season with salt pepper. Add 2 to 3 tablespoons water to create a creamy yet pourable consistency and set aside.
4. Make the Bowl
5. Preheat the oven to 425ºF. Line a baking sheet with parchment paper.
6. Place the sweet potato on the prepared baking sheet and drizzle with the olive oil. Toss well
7. Roast in the preheated oven for 10 to 15 minutes, stirring once during cooking, or until fork-tender and browned.
8. In each of 2 bowls, place ½ cup of chickpeas, 1 cup of baby kale, and half of the cooked sweet potato. Serve drizzled with half of the prepared sauce.

Nutrition Info:
- Per Serving: Calories: 323;Fat: 14.1g;Protein: 17.0g;Carbs: 36.0g.

Roasted Vegetable Medley

Servings:2
Cooking Time:65 Minutes
Ingredients:
- 1 head garlic, cloves split apart, unpeeled
- 3 tbsp olive oil
- 2 carrots, cut into strips
- ¼ lb asparagus, chopped
- ½ lb Brussels sprouts, halved
- 2 cups broccoli florets
- 1 cup cherry tomatoes
- ½ fresh lemon, sliced
- Salt and black pepper to taste

Directions:
1. Preheat oven to 375 F. Drizzle the garlic cloves with some olive oil and lightly wrap them in a small piece of foil. Place the packet in the oven and roast for 30 minutes. Place all the vegetables and the lemon slices into a large mixing bowl. Drizzle with the remaining olive oil and season with salt and pepper. Increase the oven to 400 F. Pour the vegetables on a sheet pan in a single layer, leaving the packet of garlic cloves on the pan. Roast for 20 minutes, shaking occasionally until tender. Remove the pan from the oven. Let the garlic cloves sit until cool enough to handle, then remove the skins. Top the vegetables with roasted garlic and serve.

Nutrition Info:

- Per Serving: Calories: 256;Fat: 15g;Protein: 7g;Carbs: 31g.

Simple Honey-glazed Baby Carrots

Servings:2
Cooking Time: 6 Minutes
Ingredients:

- ⅔ cup water
- 1½ pounds baby carrots
- 4 tablespoons almond butter
- ½ cup honey
- 1 teaspoon dried thyme
- 1½ teaspoons dried dill
- Salt, to taste

Directions:

1. Pour the water into the Instant Pot and add a steamer basket. Place the baby carrots in the basket.
2. Secure the lid. Select the Manual mode and set the cooking time for 4 minutes at High Pressure.
3. Once cooking is complete, do a quick pressure release. Carefully open the lid.
4. Transfer the carrots to a plate and set aside.
5. Pour the water out of the Instant Pot and dry it.
6. Press the Sauté button on the Instant Pot and heat the almond butter.
7. Stir in the honey, thyme, and dill.
8. Return the carrots to the Instant Pot and stir until well coated. Sauté for another 1 minute.
9. Taste and season with salt as needed. Serve warm.

Nutrition Info:

- Per Serving: Calories: 575;Fat: 23.5g;Protein: 2.8g;Carbs: 90.6g.

Steamed Beetroot With Nutty Yogurt

Servings:4
Cooking Time:30 Min + Chilling Time
Ingredients:

- ¼ cup extra virgin olive oil
- 1 lb beetroots, cut into wedges
- 1 cup Greek yogurt
- 3 spring onions, sliced
- 5 dill pickles, finely chopped
- 2 garlic cloves, minced
- 2 tbsp fresh parsley, chopped
- 1 oz mixed nuts, crushed
- Salt to taste

Directions:

1. In a pot over medium heat, insert a steamer basket and pour in 1 cup of water. Place in the beetroots and steam for 10-15 minutes until tender. Remove to a plate and let cool. In a bowl, combine the pickles, spring onions, garlic, salt, 3 tbsp of olive oil, Greek yogurt, and nuts and mix well. Spread the yogurt mixture on a serving plate and arrange the

beetroot wedges on top. Drizzle with the remaining olive oil and top with parsley. Serve and enjoy!

Nutrition Info:

- Per Serving: Calories: 271;Fat: 18g;Protein: 9.6g;Carbs: 22g.

Tomatoes Filled With Tabbouleh

Servings:4
Cooking Time:25 Minutes
Ingredients:

- 3 tbsp olive oil, divided
- 8 medium tomatoes
- ½ cup water
- ½ cup bulgur wheat
- 1 ½ cups minced parsley
- ⅓ cup minced fresh mint
- 2 scallions, chopped
- 1 tsp sumac
- Salt and black pepper to taste
- 1 lemon, zested

Directions:

1. Place the bulgur wheat and 2 cups of salted water in a pot and bring to a boil. Lower the heat and simmer for 10 minutes or until tender. Remove the pot from the heat and cover with a lid. Let it sit for 15 minutes.
2. Preheat the oven to 400 F. Slice off the top of each tomato and scoop out the pulp and seeds using a spoon into a sieve set over a bowl. Drain and discard any excess liquid; chop the remaining pulp and place it in a large mixing bowl. Add in parsley, mint, scallions, sumac, lemon zest, lemon juice, bulgur, pepper, and salt, and mix well.
3. Spoon the filling into the tomatoes and place the lids on top. Drizzle with olive oil and bake for 15-20 minutes until the tomatoes are tender. Serve and enjoy!

Nutrition Info:

- Per Serving: Calories: 160;Fat: 7g;Protein: 5g;Carbs: 22g.

Parsley & Olive Zucchini Bake

Servings:6
Cooking Time:1 Hour 40 Minutes
Ingredients:

- 3 tbsp olive oil
- 1 can tomatoes, diced
- 2 lb zucchinis, sliced
- 1 onion, chopped
- Salt and black pepper to taste
- 3 garlic cloves, minced
- ¼ tsp dried oregano
- ¼ tsp red pepper flakes
- 10 Kalamata olives, chopped
- 2 tbsp fresh parsley, chopped

Directions:

1. Preheat oven to 325 F. Warm the olive oil in a saucepan over medium heat. Sauté zucchini for about 3 minutes per side; transfer to a bowl. Stir-fry the onion and salt in the same saucepan for 3-5 minutes, stirring occasionally until onion soft and lightly golden. Stir in garlic, oregano, and pepper flakes and cook until fragrant, about 30 seconds.

2. Add in olives, tomatoes, salt, and pepper, bring to a simmer, and cook for about 10 minutes, stirring occasionally. Return the zucchini, cover, and transfer the pot to the oven. Bake for 10-15 minutes. Sprinkle with parsley and serve.

Nutrition Info:

- Per Serving: Calories: 164;Fat: 6g;Protein: 1.5g;Carbs: 7.7g.

Chili Vegetable Skillet

Servings:4

Cooking Time:30 Minutes

Ingredients:

- 1 cup condensed cream of mushroom soup
- 1 ½ lb eggplants, cut into chunks
- 1 cup cremini mushrooms, sliced
- 4 tbsp olive oil
- 1 carrot, thinly sliced
- 1 can tomatoes
- ½ cup red onion, thinly sliced
- 2 garlic cloves, minced
- 1 tsp fresh rosemary
- 1 tsp chili pepper
- Salt and black pepper to taste
- 2 tbsp parsley, chopped
- ¼ cup Parmesan cheese, grated

Directions:

1. Warm the olive oil in a skillet over medium heat. Add in the eggplant and cook until golden brown on all sides, about 5 minutes; set aside. Add in the carrot, onion, and mushrooms and sauté for 4 more minutes to the same skillet. Add in garlic, rosemary, and chili pepper. Cook for another 30-40 seconds. Add in 1 cup of water, cream of mushroom soup, and tomatoes. Bring to a boil and lower the heat; simmer covered for 5 minutes. Mix in sautéed eggplants and parsley and cook for 10 more minutes. Sprinkle with salt and black pepper. Serve topped with Parmesan cheese.

Nutrition Info:

- Per Serving: Calories: 261;Fat: 18.7g;Protein: 5g;Carbs: 23g.

Grilled Vegetable Skewers

Servings:4

Cooking Time: 10 Minutes

Ingredients:

- 4 medium red onions, peeled and sliced into 6 wedges
- 4 medium zucchini, cut into 1-inch-thick slices
- 2 beefsteak tomatoes, cut into quarters
- 4 red bell peppers, cut into 2-inch squares
- 2 orange bell peppers, cut into 2-inch squares
- 2 yellow bell peppers, cut into 2-inch squares
- 2 tablespoons plus 1 teaspoon olive oil, divided
- SPECIAL EQUIPMENT:
- 4 wooden skewers, soaked in water for at least 30 minutes

Directions:

1. Preheat the grill to medium-high heat.

2. Skewer the vegetables by alternating between red onion, zucchini, tomatoes, and the different colored bell peppers. Brush them with 2 tablespoons of olive oil.

3. Oil the grill grates with 1 teaspoon of olive oil and grill the vegetable skewers for 5 minutes. Flip the skewers and grill for 5 minutes more, or until they are cooked to your liking.

4. Let the skewers cool for 5 minutes before serving.

Nutrition Info:

- Per Serving: Calories: 115;Fat: 3.0g;Protein: 3.5g;Carbs: 18.7g.

Spicy Potato Wedges

Servings:4

Cooking Time:30 Minutes

Ingredients:

- 1 ½ lb potatoes, peeled and cut into wedges
- 3 tbsp olive oil
- 1 tbsp minced fresh rosemary
- 2 tsp chili powder
- 3 garlic cloves, minced
- Salt and black pepper to taste

Directions:

1. Preheat the oven to 370 F. Toss the wedges with olive oil, garlic, salt, and pepper. Spread out in a roasting sheet. Roast for 15-20 minutes until browned and crisp at the edges. Remove and sprinkle with chili powder and rosemary.

Nutrition Info:

- Per Serving: Calories: 152;Fat: 7g;Protein: 2.5g;Carbs: 21g.

Minty Broccoli & Walnuts

Servings:2

Cooking Time:10 Minutes

Ingredients:

- 1 garlic clove, minced
- ½ cups walnuts, chopped
- 3 cups broccoli florets, steamed
- 1 tbsp mint, chopped
- ½ lemon, juiced
- Salt and black pepper to taste

Directions:

1. Mix walnuts, broccoli, garlic, mint, lemon juice, salt, and pepper in a bowl. Serve chilled.

Nutrition Info:
- Per Serving: Calories: 210;Fat: 7g;Protein: 4g;Carbs: 9g.

Balsamic Grilled Vegetables

Servings:4
Cooking Time:20 Minutes
Ingredients:
- ¼ cup olive oil
- 4 carrots, cut in half
- 2 onions, quartered
- 1 zucchini, cut into rounds
- 1 eggplant, cut into rounds
- 1 red bell pepper, chopped
- Salt and black pepper to taste
- Balsamic vinegar to taste

Directions:
1. Heat your grill to medium-high. Brush the vegetables lightly with olive oil, and season with salt and pepper. Grill the vegetables for 3–4 minutes per side. Transfer to a serving dish and drizzle with balsamic vinegar. Serve and enjoy!

Nutrition Info:
- Per Serving: Calories: 184;Fat: 14g;Protein: 2.1g;Carbs: 14g.

Simple Zoodles

Servings:2
Cooking Time: 5 Minutes
Ingredients:
- 2 tablespoons avocado oil
- 2 medium zucchinis, spiralized
- ¼ teaspoon salt
- Freshly ground black pepper, to taste

Directions:
1. Heat the avocado oil in a large skillet over medium heat until it shimmers.
2. Add the zucchini noodles, salt, and black pepper to the skillet and toss to coat. Cook for 1 to 2 minutes, stirring constantly, until tender.
3. Serve warm.

Nutrition Info:
- Per Serving: Calories: 128;Fat: 14.0g;Protein: 0.3g;Carbs: 0.3g.

Simple Oven-baked Green Beans

Servings:6
Cooking Time:15 Minutes
Ingredients:
- 2 tbsp olive oil
- 2 lb green beans, trimmed
- Salt and black pepper to taste

Directions:

1. Preheat oven to 400 F. Toss the green beans with some olive oil, salt, and spread them in a single layer on a greased baking dish. Roast for 8-10 minutes. Transfer green beans to a serving platter and drizzle with the remaining olive oil.

Nutrition Info:
- Per Serving: Calories: 157;Fat: 2g;Protein: 3g;Carbs: 6g.

Wilted Dandelion Greens With Sweet Onion

Servings:4
Cooking Time: 15 Minutes
Ingredients:
- 1 tablespoon extra-virgin olive oil
- 2 garlic cloves, minced
- 1 Vidalia onion, thinly sliced
- ½ cup low-sodium vegetable broth
- 2 bunches dandelion greens, roughly chopped
- Freshly ground black pepper, to taste

Directions:
1. Heat the olive oil in a large skillet over low heat.
2. Add the garlic and onion and cook for 2 to 3 minutes, stirring occasionally, or until the onion is translucent.
3. Fold in the vegetable broth and dandelion greens and cook for 5 to 7 minutes until wilted, stirring frequently.
4. Sprinkle with the black pepper and serve on a plate while warm.

Nutrition Info:
- Per Serving: Calories: 81;Fat: 3.9g;Protein: 3.2g;Carbs: 10.8g.

Beet And Watercress Salad

Servings:4
Cooking Time: 8 Minutes
Ingredients:
- 2 pounds beets, scrubbed, trimmed and cut into ¾-inch pieces
- ½ cup water
- 1 teaspoon caraway seeds
- ½ teaspoon table salt, plus more for seasoning
- 1 cup plain Greek yogurt
- 1 small garlic clove, minced
- 5 ounces watercress, torn into bite-size pieces
- 1 tablespoon extra-virgin olive oil, divided, plus more for drizzling
- 1 tablespoon white wine vinegar, divided
- Black pepper, to taste
- 1 teaspoon grated orange zest
- 2 tablespoons orange juice
- ¼ cup coarsely chopped fresh dill
- ¼ cup hazelnuts, toasted, skinned and chopped
- Coarse sea salt, to taste

Directions:

1. Combine the beets, water, caraway seeds and table salt in the Instant Pot. Set the lid in place. Select the Manual mode and set the cooking time for 8 minutes on High Pressure. When the timer goes off, do a quick pressure release.

2. Carefully open the lid. Using a slotted spoon, transfer the beets to a plate. Set aside to cool slightly.

3. In a small bowl, combine the yogurt, garlic and 3 tablespoons of the beet cooking liquid. In a large bowl, toss the watercress with 2 teaspoons of the oil and 1 teaspoon of the vinegar. Season with table salt and pepper.

4. Spread the yogurt mixture over a serving dish. Arrange the watercress on top of the yogurt mixture, leaving 1-inch border of the yogurt mixture.

5. Add the beets to now-empty large bowl and toss with the orange zest and juice, the remaining 2 teaspoons of the vinegar and the remaining 1 teaspoon of the oil. Season with table salt and pepper.

6. Arrange the beets on top of the watercress mixture. Drizzle with the olive oil and sprinkle with the dill, hazelnuts and sea salt.

7. Serve immediately.

Nutrition Info:

- Per Serving: Calories: 240;Fat: 15.0g;Protein: 9.0g;Carbs: 19.0g.

Celery And Mustard Greens

Servings:4
Cooking Time: 15 Minutes

Ingredients:

- ½ cup low-sodium vegetable broth
- 1 celery stalk, roughly chopped
- ½ sweet onion, chopped
- ½ large red bell pepper, thinly sliced
- 2 garlic cloves, minced
- 1 bunch mustard greens, roughly chopped

Directions:

1. Pour the vegetable broth into a large cast iron pan and bring it to a simmer over medium heat.

2. Stir in the celery, onion, bell pepper, and garlic. Cook uncovered for about 3 to 5 minutes, or until the onion is softened.

3. Add the mustard greens to the pan and stir well. Cover, reduce the heat to low, and cook for an additional 10 minutes, or until the liquid is evaporated and the greens are wilted.

4. Remove from the heat and serve warm.

Nutrition Info:

- Per Serving: Calories: 39;Fat: 0g;Protein: 3.1g;Carbs: 6.8g.

Tradicional Matchuba Green Beans

Servings:4

Cooking Time:15 Minutes

Ingredients:

- 1 ¼ lb narrow green beans, trimmed
- 3 tbsp butter, melted
- 1 cup Moroccan matbucha
- 2 green onions, chopped
- Salt and black pepper to taste

Directions:

1. Steam the green beans in a pot for 5-6 minutes until tender. Remove to a bowl, reserving the cooking liquid. In a skillet over medium heat, melt the butter. Add in green onions, salt, and black pepper and cook until fragrant. Lower the heat and put in the green beans along with some of the reserved water. Simmer for 3-4 minutes. Serve the green beans with the Sabra Moroccan matbucha as a dip.

Nutrition Info:

- Per Serving: Calories: 125;Fat: 8.6g;Protein: 2.2g;Carbs: 9g.

Chickpea Lettuce Wraps With Celery

Servings:4
Cooking Time: 0 Minutes

Ingredients:

- 1 can low-sodium chickpeas, drained and rinsed
- 1 celery stalk, thinly sliced
- 2 tablespoons finely chopped red onion
- 2 tablespoons unsalted tahini
- 3 tablespoons honey mustard
- 1 tablespoon capers, undrained
- 12 butter lettuce leaves

Directions:

1. In a bowl, mash the chickpeas with a potato masher or the back of a fork until mostly smooth.

2. Add the celery, red onion, tahini, honey mustard, and capers to the bowl and stir until well incorporated.

3. For each serving, place three overlapping lettuce leaves on a plate and top with ¼ of the mashed chickpea filling, then roll up. Repeat with the remaining lettuce leaves and chickpea mixture.

Nutrition Info:

- Per Serving: Calories: 182;Fat: 7.1g;Protein: 10.3g;Carbs: 19.6g.

Garlicky Zucchini Cubes With Mint

Servings:4
Cooking Time: 10 Minutes

Ingredients:

- 3 large green zucchinis, cut into ½-inch cubes
- 3 tablespoons extra-virgin olive oil
- 1 large onion, chopped
- 3 cloves garlic, minced
- 1 teaspoon salt

- 1 teaspoon dried mint

Directions:

1. Heat the olive oil in a large skillet over medium heat.
2. Add the onion and garlic and sauté for 3 minutes, stirring constantly, or until softened.
3. Stir in the zucchini cubes and salt and cook for 5 minutes, or until the zucchini is browned and tender.
4. Add the mint to the skillet and toss to combine, then continue cooking for 2 minutes.
5. Serve warm.

Nutrition Info:

- Per Serving: Calories: 146;Fat: 10.6g;Protein: 4.2g;Carbs: 11.8g.

Roasted Veggies And Brown Rice Bowl

Servings:4

Cooking Time: 20 Minutes

Ingredients:

- 2 cups cauliflower florets
- 2 cups broccoli florets
- 1 can chickpeas, drained and rinsed
- 1 cup carrot slices
- 2 to 3 tablespoons extra-virgin olive oil, divided
- Salt and freshly ground black pepper, to taste
- Nonstick cooking spray
- 2 cups cooked brown rice
- 2 to 3 tablespoons sesame seeds, for garnish
- Dressing:
- 3 to 4 tablespoons tahini
- 2 tablespoons honey
- 1 lemon, juiced
- 1 garlic clove, minced
- Salt and freshly ground black pepper, to taste

Directions:

1. Preheat the oven to 400ºF. Spritz two baking sheets with nonstick cooking spray.
2. Spread the cauliflower and broccoli on the first baking sheet and the second with the chickpeas and carrot slices.
3. Drizzle each sheet with half of the olive oil and sprinkle with salt and pepper. Toss to coat well.
4. Roast the chickpeas and carrot slices in the preheated oven for 10 minutes, leaving the carrots tender but crisp, and the cauliflower and broccoli for 20 minutes until fork-tender. Stir them once halfway through the cooking time.
5. Meanwhile, make the dressing: Whisk together the tahini, honey, lemon juice, garlic, salt, and pepper in a small bowl.
6. Divide the cooked brown rice among four bowls. Top each bowl evenly with roasted vegetables and dressing. Sprinkle the sesame seeds on top for garnish before serving.

Nutrition Info:

- Per Serving: Calories: 453;Fat: 17.8g;Protein: 12.1g;Carbs: 61.8g.

Roasted Artichokes

Servings:4

Cooking Time:50 Minutes

Ingredients:

- 4 artichokes, stalk trimmed and large leaves removed
- 2 lemons, freshly squeezed
- 4 tbsp extra-virgin olive oil
- 4 cloves garlic, chopped
- 1 tsp fresh rosemary
- 1 tsp fresh basil
- 1 tsp fresh parsley
- 1 tsp fresh oregano
- Salt and black pepper to taste
- 1 tsp red pepper flakes
- 1 tsp paprika

Directions:

1. Preheat oven to 395 F. In a small bowl, thoroughly combine the garlic with herbs and spices; set aside. Cut the artichokes in half vertically and scoop out the fibrous choke to expose the heart with a teaspoon.
2. Rub the lemon juice all over the entire surface of the artichoke halves. Arrange them on a parchment-lined baking dish, cut side up, and brush them evenly with olive oil. Stuff the cavities with the garlic/herb mixture. Cover them with aluminum foil and bake for 30 minutes. Discard the foil and bake for another 10 minutes until lightly charred. Serve.

Nutrition Info:

- Per Serving: Calories: 220;Fat: 14g;Protein: 6g;Carbs: 21g.

Mushroom & Cauliflower Roast

Servings:4

Cooking Time:35 Minutes

Ingredients:

- 2 tbsp olive oil
- 4 cups cauliflower florets
- 1 celery stalk, chopped
- 1 cup mushrooms, sliced
- 10 cherry tomatoes, halved
- 1 yellow onion, chopped
- 2 garlic cloves, minced
- 2 tbsp dill, chopped
- Salt and black pepper to taste

Directions:

1. Preheat the oven to 340 F. Line a baking sheet with parchment paper. Place in cauliflower florets, olive oil, mushrooms, celery, tomatoes, onion, garlic, salt, and pepper and mix to combine. Bake for 25 minutes. Serve topped with dill.

Nutrition Info:

- Per Serving: Calories: 380;Fat: 15g;Protein: 12g;Carbs: 17g.

Chargrilled Vegetable Kebabs

Servings:4
Cooking Time:26 Minutes
Ingredients:
- 2 red bell peppers, cut into squares
- 2 zucchinis, sliced into half-moons
- 6 portobello mushroom caps, quartered
- ¼ cup olive oil
- 1 tsp Dijon mustard
- 1 tsp fresh rosemary, chopped
- 1 garlic clove, minced
- Salt and black pepper to taste
- 2 red onions, cut into wedges

Directions:
1. Preheat your grill to High. Mix the olive oil, mustard, rosemary, garlic, salt, and pepper in a bowl. Reserve half of the oil mixture for serving. Thread the vegetables in alternating order onto metal skewers and brush them with the remaining oil mixture. Grill them for about 15 minutes until browned, turning occasionally. Transfer the kebabs to a serving platter and remove the skewers. Drizzle with reserved oil mixture and serve.

Nutrition Info:
- Per Serving: Calories: 96;Fat: 9.2g;Protein: 1.1g;Carbs: 3.6g.

Grilled Za´atar Zucchini Rounds

Servings:4
Cooking Time:20 Minutes
Ingredients:
- 2 tbsp olive oil
- 4 zucchinis, sliced
- 1 tbsp za'atar seasoning
- Salt to taste
- 2 tbsp parsley, chopped

Directions:
1. Preheat the grill on high. Cut the zucchini lengthways into ½-inch thin pieces. Brush the zucchini 'steaks' with olive oil and season with salt and za'atar seasoning. Grill for 6 minutes on both sides. Sprinkle with parsley and serve.

Nutrition Info:
- Per Serving: Calories: 91;Fat: 7.4g;Protein: 2.4g;Carbs: 6.6g.

Spanish-style Green Beans With Pine Nuts

Servings:6
Cooking Time:30 Minutes
Ingredients:
- ¼ cup Manchego cheese, shredded
- ¼ cup olive oil
- 2 lb green beans, trimmed
- Salt and black pepper to taste
- 2 garlic cloves, minced
- 1 tsp Dijon mustard
- 2 tbsp fresh parsley, chopped
- 2 tbsp pine nuts, toasted

Directions:
1. Preheat oven to 420 F. Toss green beans with some olive oil, salt, and pepper. Transfer to a baking sheet and roast for 15-18 minutes, shaking occasionally the sheet. Transfer green beans to a serving plate. Microwave mixed garlic, lemon zest, salt, pepper, and the remaining olive oil for about 1 minute until bubbling. Let the mixture sit for 1 minute, then whisk in lemon juice, mustard, salt, and pepper. Drizzle the green beans with the dressing and sprinkle with basil. Top with cheese and pine nuts. Serve and enjoy!

Nutrition Info:
- Per Serving: Calories: 126;Fat: 11g;Protein: 2.6g;Carbs: 6.3g.

Balsamic Cherry Tomatoes

Servings:4
Cooking Time:10 Minutes
Ingredients:
- 2 tbsp olive oil
- 2 lb cherry tomatoes, halved
- 2 tbsp balsamic glaze
- Salt and black pepper to taste
- 1 garlic clove, minced
- 2 tbsp fresh basil, torn

Directions:
1. Warm the olive oil in a skillet over medium heat. Add the cherry tomatoes and cook for 1-2 minutes, stirring occasionally. Stir in garlic, salt, and pepper and cook until fragrant, about 30 seconds. Drizzle with balsamic glaze and decorate with basil. Serve and enjoy!

Nutrition Info:
- Per Serving: Calories: 45;Fat: 2.5g;Protein: 1.1g;Carbs: 5.6g.

Baked Vegetable Stew

Servings:6
Cooking Time:70 Minutes
Ingredients:
- 1 can diced tomatoes, drained with juice reserved
- 3 tbsp olive oil
- 1 onion, chopped
- 2 tbsp fresh oregano, minced
- 1 tsp paprika
- 4 garlic cloves, minced
- 1 ½ lb green beans, sliced
- 1 lb Yukon Gold potatoes, peeled and chopped

- 1 tbsp tomato paste
- Salt and black pepper to taste
- 3 tbsp fresh basil, chopped

Directions:

1. Preheat oven to 360 F. Warm the olive oil in a skillet over medium heat. Sauté onion and garlic for 3 minutes until softened. Stir in oregano and paprika for 30 seconds. Transfer to a baking dish and add in green beans, potatoes, tomatoes, tomato paste, salt, pepper, and 1 ½ cups of water; stir well. Bake for 40-50 minutes. Sprinkle with basil. Serve.

Nutrition Info:

- Per Serving: Calories: 121;Fat: 0.8g;Protein: 4.2g;Carbs: 26g.

Baked Potato With Veggie Mix

Servings:4
Cooking Time:45 Minutes
Ingredients:

- 4 tbsp olive oil
- 1 lb potatoes, peeled and diced
- 2 red bell peppers, halved
- 1 lb mushrooms, sliced
- 2 tomatoes, diced
- 8 garlic cloves, peeled
- 1 eggplant, sliced
- 1 yellow onion, quartered
- ½ tsp dried oregano
- ¼ tsp caraway seeds
- Salt to taste

Directions:

1. Preheat the oven to 390 F. In a bowl, combine the bell peppers, mushrooms, tomatoes, eggplant, onion, garlic, salt, olive oil, oregano, and caraway seeds. Set aside. Arrange the potatoes on a baking dish and bake for 15 minutes. Top with the veggies mixture and bake for 15-20 minutes until tender.

Nutrition Info:

- Per Serving: Calories: 302;Fat: 15g;Protein: 8.5g;Carbs: 39g.

Moroccan Tagine With Vegetables

Servings:2
Cooking Time: 40 Minutes
Ingredients:

- 2 tablespoons olive oil
- ½ onion, diced
- 1 garlic clove, minced
- 2 cups cauliflower florets
- 1 medium carrot, cut into 1-inch pieces
- 1 cup diced eggplant
- 1 can whole tomatoes with their juices
- 1 can chickpeas, drained and rinsed
- 2 small red potatoes, cut into 1-inch pieces
- 1 cup water

- 1 teaspoon pure maple syrup
- ½ teaspoon cinnamon
- ½ teaspoon turmeric
- 1 teaspoon cumin
- ½ teaspoon salt
- 1 to 2 teaspoons harissa paste

Directions:

1. In a Dutch oven, heat the olive oil over medium-high heat. Sauté the onion for 5 minutes, stirring occasionally, or until the onion is translucent.

2. Stir in the garlic, cauliflower florets, carrot, eggplant, tomatoes, and potatoes. Using a wooden spoon or spatula to break up the tomatoes into smaller pieces.

3. Add the chickpeas, water, maple syrup, cinnamon, turmeric, cumin, and salt and stir to incorporate. Bring the mixture to a boil.

4. Once it starts to boil, reduce the heat to medium-low. Stir in the harissa paste, cover, allow to simmer for about 40 minutes, or until the vegetables are softened. Taste and adjust seasoning as needed.

5. Let the mixture cool for 5 minutes before serving.

Nutrition Info:

- Per Serving: Calories: 293;Fat: 9.9g;Protein: 11.2g;Carbs: 45.5g.

Homemade Vegetarian Moussaka

Servings:4
Cooking Time:80 Minutes
Ingredients:

- 2 tbsp olive oil
- 1 yellow onion, chopped
- 2 garlic cloves, chopped
- 2 eggplants, halved
- ½ cup vegetable broth
- Salt and black pepper to taste
- ½ tsp paprika
- ¼ cup parsley, chopped
- 1 tsp basil, chopped
- 1 tsp hot sauce
- 1 tomato, chopped
- 2 tbsp tomato puree
- 6 Kalamata olives, chopped
- ½ cup feta cheese, crumbled

Directions:

1. Preheat oven to 360 F. Remove the tender center part of the eggplants and chop it. Arrange the eggplant halves on a baking tray and drizzle with some olive oil. Roast for 35-40 minutes.

2. Warm the remaining olive oil in a skillet over medium heat and add eggplant flesh, onion, and garlic and sauté for 5 minutes until tender. Stir in the vegetable broth, salt, pepper, basil, hot sauce, paprika, tomato, and tomato puree. Lower the heat and simmer for 10-15 minutes. Once the eggplants

are ready, remove them from the oven and fill them with the mixture. Top with Kalamata olives and feta cheese. Return to the oven and bake for 10-15 minutes. Sprinkle with parsley.

Nutrition Info:
- Per Serving: Calories: 223;Fat: 14g;Protein: 6.9g;Carbs: 23g.

5-ingredient Zucchini Fritters

Servings:14
Cooking Time: 5 Minutes
Ingredients:
- 4 cups grated zucchini
- Salt, to taste
- 2 large eggs, lightly beaten
- ⅓ cup sliced scallions (green and white parts)
- ⅔ all-purpose flour
- ⅛ teaspoon black pepper
- 2 tablespoons olive oil

Directions:
1. Put the grated zucchini in a colander and lightly season with salt. Set aside to rest for 10 minutes. Squeeze out as much liquid from the grated zucchini as possible.
2. Pour the grated zucchini into a bowl. Fold in the beaten eggs, scallions, flour, salt, and pepper and stir until everything is well combined.
3. Heat the olive oil in a large skillet over medium heat until hot.
4. Drop 3 tablespoons mounds of the zucchini mixture onto the hot skillet to make each fritter, pressing them lightly into rounds and spacing them about 2 inches apart.
5. Cook for 2 to 3 minutes. Flip the zucchini fritters and cook for 2 minutes more, or until they are golden brown and cooked through.
6. Remove from the heat to a plate lined with paper towels. Repeat with the remaining zucchini mixture.
7. Serve hot.

Nutrition Info:
- Per Serving: Calories: 113;Fat: 6.1g;Protein: 4.0g;Carbs: 12.2g.

Fried Eggplant Rolls

Servings:4
Cooking Time: 10 Minutes
Ingredients:
- 2 large eggplants, trimmed and cut lengthwise into ¼-inch-thick slices
- 1 teaspoon salt
- 1 cup shredded ricotta cheese
- 4 ounces goat cheese, shredded
- ¼ cup finely chopped fresh basil
- ½ teaspoon freshly ground black pepper
- Olive oil spray

Directions:

1. Add the eggplant slices to a colander and season with salt. Set aside for 15 to 20 minutes.
2. Mix together the ricotta and goat cheese, basil, and black pepper in a large bowl and stir to combine. Set aside.
3. Dry the eggplant slices with paper towels and lightly mist them with olive oil spray.
4. Heat a large skillet over medium heat and lightly spray it with olive oil spray.
5. Arrange the eggplant slices in the skillet and fry each side for 3 minutes until golden brown.
6. Remove from the heat to a paper towel-lined plate and rest for 5 minutes.
7. Make the eggplant rolls: Lay the eggplant slices on a flat work surface and top each slice with a tablespoon of the prepared cheese mixture. Roll them up and serve immediately.

Nutrition Info:
- Per Serving: Calories: 254;Fat: 14.9g;Protein: 15.3g;Carbs: 18.6g.

Veggie-stuffed Portabello Mushrooms

Servings:6
Cooking Time: 24 To 25 Minutes
Ingredients:
- 3 tablespoons extra-virgin olive oil, divided
- 1 cup diced onion
- 2 garlic cloves, minced
- 1 large zucchini, diced
- 3 cups chopped mushrooms
- 1 cup chopped tomato
- 1 teaspoon dried oregano
- ¼ teaspoon kosher salt
- ¼ teaspoon crushed red pepper
- 6 large portabello mushrooms, stems and gills removed
- Cooking spray
- 4 ounces fresh Mozzarella cheese, shredded

Directions:
1. In a large skillet over medium heat, heat 2 tablespoons of the oil. Add the onion and sauté for 4 minutes. Stir in the garlic and sauté for 1 minute.
2. Stir in the zucchini, mushrooms, tomato, oregano, salt and red pepper. Cook for 10 minutes, stirring constantly. Remove from the heat.
3. Meanwhile, heat a grill pan over medium-high heat.
4. Brush the remaining 1 tablespoon of the oil over the portabello mushroom caps. Place the mushrooms, bottom-side down, on the grill pan. Cover with a sheet of aluminum foil sprayed with nonstick cooking spray. Cook for 5 minutes.
5. Flip the mushroom caps over, and spoon about ½ cup of the cooked vegetable mixture into each cap. Top each with about 2½ tablespoons of the Mozzarella.

6. Cover and grill for 4 to 5 minutes, or until the cheese is melted.

7. Using a spatula, transfer the portabello mushrooms to a plate. Let cool for about 5 minutes before serving.

Nutrition Info:

- Per Serving: Calories: 111;Fat: 4.0g;Protein: 11.0g;Carbs: 11.0g.

Vegetable And Red Lentil Stew

Servings:6

Cooking Time: 35 Minutes

Ingredients:

- 1 tablespoon extra-virgin olive oil
- 2 onions, peeled and finely diced
- 6½ cups water
- 2 zucchinis, finely diced
- 4 celery stalks, finely diced
- 3 cups red lentils
- 1 teaspoon dried oregano
- 1 teaspoon salt, plus more as needed

Directions:

1. Heat the olive oil in a large pot over medium heat.

2. Add the onions and sauté for about 5 minutes, stirring constantly, or until the onions are softened.

3. Stir in the water, zucchini, celery, lentils, oregano, and salt and bring the mixture to a boil.

4. Reduce the heat to low and let simmer covered for 30 minutes, stirring occasionally, or until the lentils are tender.

5. Taste and adjust the seasoning as needed.

Nutrition Info:

- Per Serving: Calories: 387;Fat: 4.4g;Protein: 24.0g;Carbs: 63.7g.

Spicy Roasted Tomatoes

Servings:2

Cooking Time:50 Minutes

Ingredients:

- ¼ cup olive oil
- 1 lb mixed cherry tomatoes
- 10 garlic cloves, minced
- Salt to taste
- 1 fresh rosemary sprig
- 1 fresh thyme sprig
- 2 crusty bread slices

Directions:

1. Preheat oven to 350 F. Toss the cherry tomatoes, garlic, olive oil, and salt in a baking dish. Top with the herb sprigs. Roast the tomatoes for about 45 minutes until they are soft and begin to caramelize. Discard the herbs and serve with bread.

Nutrition Info:

- Per Serving: Calories: 271;Fat: 26g;Protein: 3g;Carbs: 12g.

Baked Honey Acorn Squash

Servings:4

Cooking Time:35 Minutes

Ingredients:

- 1 acorn squash, cut into wedges
- 2 tbsp olive oil
- 2 tbsp honey
- 2 tbsp rosemary, chopped
- 2 tbsp walnuts, chopped

Directions:

1. Preheat oven to 400 F. In a bowl, mix honey, rosemary, and olive oil. Lay the squash wedges on a baking sheet and drizzle with the honey mixture. Bake for 30 minutes until squash is tender and slightly caramelized, turning each slice over halfway through. Serve cooled sprinkled with walnuts.

Nutrition Info:

- Per Serving: Calories: 136;Fat: 6g;Protein: 0.9g;Carbs: 20g.

Stuffed Portobello Mushroom With Tomatoes

Servings:4

Cooking Time: 15 Minutes

Ingredients:

- 4 large portobello mushroom caps
- 3 tablespoons extra-virgin olive oil
- Salt and freshly ground black pepper, to taste
- 4 sun-dried tomatoes
- 1 cup shredded mozzarella cheese, divided
- ½ to ¾ cup low-sodium tomato sauce

Directions:

1. Preheat the broiler on high.

2. Arrange the mushroom caps on a baking sheet and drizzle with olive oil. Sprinkle with salt and pepper.

3. Broil for 1o minutes, flipping the mushroom caps halfway through, until browned on the top.

4. Remove from the broil. Spoon 1 tomato, 2 tablespoons of cheese, and 2 to 3 tablespoons of sauce onto each mushroom cap.

5. Return the mushroom caps to the broiler and continue broiling for 2 to 3 minutes.

6. Cool for 5 minutes before serving.

Nutrition Info:

- Per Serving: Calories: 217;Fat: 15.8g;Protein: 11.2g;Carbs: 11.7g.

Veggie Rice Bowls With Pesto Sauce

Servings:2
Cooking Time: 1 Minute
Ingredients:

- 2 cups water
- 1 cup arborio rice, rinsed
- Salt and ground black pepper, to taste
- 2 eggs
- 1 cup broccoli florets
- ½ pound Brussels sprouts
- 1 carrot, peeled and chopped
- 1 small beet, peeled and cubed
- ¼ cup pesto sauce
- Lemon wedges, for serving

Directions:

1. Combine the water, rice, salt, and pepper in the Instant Pot. Insert a trivet over rice and place a steamer basket on top. Add the eggs, broccoli, Brussels sprouts, carrots, beet cubes, salt, and pepper to the steamer basket.
2. Lock the lid. Select the Manual mode and set the cooking time for 1 minute at High Pressure.
3. When the timer beeps, perform a natural pressure release for 10 minutes, then release any remaining pressure. Carefully open the lid.
4. Remove the steamer basket and trivet from the pot and transfer the eggs to a bowl of ice water. Peel and halve the eggs. Use a fork to fluff the rice.
5. Divide the rice, broccoli, Brussels sprouts, carrot, beet cubes, and eggs into two bowls. Top with a dollop of pesto sauce and serve with the lemon wedges.

Nutrition Info:

- Per Serving: Calories: 590;Fat: 34.1g;Protein: 21.9g;Carbs: 50.0g.

Sautéed Cabbage With Parsley

Servings:4
Cooking Time: 12 To 14 Minutes
Ingredients:

- 1 small head green cabbage, cored and sliced thin
- 2 tablespoons extra-virgin olive oil, divided
- 1 onion, halved and sliced thin
- ¾ teaspoon salt, divided
- ¼ teaspoon black pepper
- ¼ cup chopped fresh parsley
- 1½ teaspoons lemon juice

Directions:

1. Place the cabbage in a large bowl with cold water. Let sit for 3 minutes. Drain well.
2. Heat 1 tablespoon of the oil in a skillet over medium-high heat until shimmering. Add the onion and ¼ teaspoon of the salt and cook for 5 to 7 minutes, or until softened and lightly browned. Transfer to a bowl.
3. Heat the remaining 1 tablespoon of the oil in now-empty skillet over medium-high heat until shimmering. Add the cabbage and sprinkle with the remaining ½ teaspoon of the salt and black pepper. Cover and cook for about 3 minutes, without stirring, or until cabbage is wilted and lightly browned on bottom.
4. Stir and continue to cook for about 4 minutes, uncovered, or until the cabbage is crisp-tender and lightly browned in places, stirring once halfway through cooking. Off heat, stir in the cooked onion, parsley and lemon juice.
5. Transfer to a plate and serve.

Nutrition Info:

- Per Serving: Calories: 117;Fat: 7.0g;Protein: 2.7g;Carbs: 13.4g.

Sautéed Spinach And Leeks

Servings:2
Cooking Time: 8 Minutes
Ingredients:

- 3 tablespoons olive oil
- 2 garlic cloves, crushed
- 2 leeks, chopped
- 2 red onions, chopped
- 9 ounces fresh spinach
- 1 teaspoon kosher salt
- ½ cup crumbled goat cheese

Directions:

1. Coat the bottom of the Instant Pot with the olive oil.
2. Add the garlic, leek, and onions and stir-fry for about 5 minutes, on Sauté mode.
3. Stir in the spinach. Sprinkle with the salt and sauté for an additional 3 minutes, stirring constantly.
4. Transfer to a plate and scatter with the goat cheese before serving.

Nutrition Info:

- Per Serving: Calories: 447;Fat: 31.2g;Protein: 14.6g;Carbs: 28.7g.

Beans , Grains, And Pastas Recipes

Cherry, Apricot, And Pecan Brown Rice Bowl

Servings:2
Cooking Time: 1 Hour 1 Minutes
Ingredients:
- 2 tablespoons olive oil
- 2 green onions, sliced
- ½ cup brown rice
- 1 cup low -sodium chicken stock
- 2 tablespoons dried cherries
- 4 dried apricots, chopped
- 2 tablespoons pecans, toasted and chopped
- Sea salt and freshly ground pepper, to taste

Directions:
1. Heat the olive oil in a medium saucepan over medium-high heat until shimmering.
2. Add the green onions and sauté for 1 minutes or until fragrant.
3. Add the rice. Stir to mix well, then pour in the chicken stock.
4. Bring to a boil. Reduce the heat to low. Cover and simmer for 50 minutes or until the brown rice is soft.
5. Add the cherries, apricots, and pecans, and simmer for 10 more minutes or until the fruits are tender.
6. Pour them in a large serving bowl. Fluff with a fork. Sprinkle with sea salt and freshly ground pepper. Serve immediately.

Nutrition Info:
- Per Serving: Calories: 451;Fat: 25.9g;Protein: 8.2g;Carbs: 50.4g.

Broccoli And Carrot Pasta Salad

Servings:2
Cooking Time: 10 Minutes
Ingredients:
- 8 ounces whole-wheat pasta
- 2 cups broccoli florets
- 1 cup peeled and shredded carrots
- ¼ cup plain Greek yogurt
- Juice of 1 lemon
- 1 teaspoon red pepper flakes
- Sea salt and freshly ground pepper, to taste

Directions:
1. Bring a large pot of lightly salted water to a boil. Add the pasta to the boiling water and cook until al dente. Drain and let rest for a few minutes.
2. When cooled, combine the pasta with the veggies, yogurt, lemon juice, and red pepper flakes in a large bowl, and stir thoroughly to combine.

3. Taste and season to taste with salt and pepper. Serve immediately.

Nutrition Info:
- Per Serving: Calories: 428;Fat: 2.9g;Protein: 15.9g;Carbs: 84.6g.

Lemony Tuna Barley With Capers

Servings:4
Cooking Time:50 Minutes
Ingredients:
- 2 tbsp olive oil
- 3 cups chicken stock
- 10 oz canned tuna, flaked
- 1 cup barley
- Salt and black pepper to taste
- 12 cherry tomatoes, halved
- ½ cup pepperoncini, sliced
- ¼ cup capers, drained
- ½ lemon, juiced

Directions:
1. Boil chicken stock in a saucepan over medium heat and add in barley. Cook covered for 40 minutes. Fluff the barley and remove to a bowl. Stir in tuna, salt, pepper, tomatoes, pepperoncini, olive oil, capers, and lemon juice. Serve.

Nutrition Info:
- Per Serving: Calories: 260;Fat: 12g;Protein: 24g;Carbs: 17g.

Brown Rice Pilaf With Pistachios And Raisins

Servings:6
Cooking Time: 15 Minutes
Ingredients:
- 1 tablespoon extra-virgin olive oil
- 1 cup chopped onion
- ½ cup shredded carrot
- ½ teaspoon ground cinnamon
- 1 teaspoon ground cumin
- 2 cups brown rice
- 1¾ cups pure orange juice
- ¼ cup water
- ½ cup shelled pistachios
- 1 cup golden raisins
- ½ cup chopped fresh chives

Directions:
1. Heat the olive oil in a saucepan over medium-high heat until shimmering.
2. Add the onion and sauté for 5 minutes or until translucent.

45

3. Add the carrots, cinnamon, and cumin, then sauté for 1 minutes or until aromatic.

4. Pour int the brown rice, orange juice, and water. Bring to a boil. Reduce the heat to medium-low and simmer for 7 minutes or until the liquid is almost absorbed.

5. Transfer the rice mixture in a large serving bowl, then spread with pistachios, raisins, and chives. Serve immediately.

Nutrition Info:

- Per Serving: Calories: 264;Fat: 7.1g;Protein: 5.2g;Carbs: 48.9g.

Simple Lentil Risotto

Servings:2

Cooking Time: 20 Minutes

Ingredients:

- ½ tablespoon olive oil
- ½ medium onion, chopped
- ½ cup dry lentils, soaked overnight
- ½ celery stalk, chopped
- 1 sprig parsley, chopped
- ½ cup Arborio (short-grain Italian) rice
- 1 garlic clove, lightly mashed
- 2 cups vegetable stock

Directions:

1. Press the Sauté button to heat your Instant Pot.

2. Add the oil and onion to the Instant Pot and sauté for 5 minutes.

3. Add all the remaining ingredients to the Instant Pot.

4. Secure the lid. Select the Manual mode and set the cooking time for 15 minutes at High Pressure.

5. Once cooking is complete, do a natural pressure release for 20 minutes, then release any remaining pressure. Carefully open the lid.

6. Stir and serve hot.

Nutrition Info:

- Per Serving: Calories: 261;Fat: 3.6g;Protein: 10.6g;Carbs: 47.1g.

Herb Bean Stew

Servings:4

Cooking Time:70 Minutes

Ingredients:

- 2 tbsp olive oil
- 3 tomatoes, cubed
- 1 yellow onion, chopped
- 1 celery stalk, chopped
- 2 tbsp parsley, chopped
- 2 garlic cloves, minced
- 1 cup lima beans, soaked
- 1 tsp paprika
- 1 tsp dried oregano
- ½ tsp dried thyme

- Salt and black pepper to taste

Directions:

1. Cover the lima beans with water in a pot and place over medium heat. Bring to a boil and cook for 30 minutes. Drain and set aside. Warm olive oil in the pot over medium heat and cook onion and garlic for 3 minutes. Stir in tomatoes, celery, oregano, thyme, and paprika and cook for 5 minutes. Pour in 3 cups of water and return the lima beans; season with salt and pepper. Simmer for 30 minutes. Top with parsley.

Nutrition Info:

- Per Serving: Calories: 310;Fat: 16g;Protein: 16g;Carbs: 30g.

Arroz Con Pollo

Servings:4

Cooking Time:50 Minutes

Ingredients:

- 2 tbsp olive oil
- 1 lb chicken thighs, skinless
- 1 cup Spanish rice
- 2 cups chicken broth
- ½ cup spring onions, chopped
- ½ red bell pepper, chopped
- ¼ cup tomato paste
- 2 garlic cloves, minced
- ¼ cup white wine
- ½ tsp sweet paprika
- ¼ tsp turmeric
- ½ tsp dried basil
- ½ tsp dried tarragon
- Salt and black pepper to taste

Directions:

1. Warm the olive oil in a saucepan over medium heat and stir-fry the chicken for 8-10 minutes. Remove to a plate to cool. Add spring onions, bell pepper, and garlic to the saucepan and cook for 3 minutes. Pour in white wine to scrape off any bits from the bottom. Discard the bones from the chicken and shred it with a fork. Return to the saucepan and sprinkle with salt, black pepper, paprika, turmeric, tarragon, and basil. Stir in the rice, tomato paste, and chicken broth. Cook covered for about 20 minutes. Serve and enjoy!

Nutrition Info:

- Per Serving: Calories: 502;Fat: 17g;Protein: 39g;Carbs: 44g.

Quick Pesto Pasta

Servings:4
Cooking Time:20 Minutes
Ingredients:

- 1 lb linguine
- 2 tomatoes, chopped
- 10 oz basil pesto
- ½ cup pine nuts, toasted
- ½ cup Parmesan cheese, grated
- 1 lemon, zested

Directions:

1. Bring to a boil salted water in a pot over high heat. Add the linguine and cook according to package directions, 9-11 minutes. Drain and transfer to a serving bowl. Add the tomatoes, pesto, and lemon zest toss gently to coat the pasta. Sprinkle with Parmesan cheese and pine nuts and serve.

Nutrition Info:

- Per Serving: Calories: 617;Fat: 17g;Protein: 23g;Carbs: 94g.

Lentil And Mushroom Pasta

Servings:2
Cooking Time: 50 Minutes
Ingredients:

- 2 tablespoons olive oil
- 1 large yellow onion, finely diced
- 2 portobello mushrooms, trimmed and chopped finely
- 2 tablespoons tomato paste
- 3 garlic cloves, chopped
- 1 teaspoon oregano
- 2½ cups water
- 1 cup brown lentils
- 1 can diced tomatoes with basil (with juice if diced)
- 1 tablespoon balsamic vinegar
- 8 ounces pasta of choice, cooked
- Salt and black pepper, to taste
- Chopped basil, for garnish

Directions:

1. Place a large stockpot over medium heat. Add the oil. Once the oil is hot, add the onion and mushrooms. Cover and cook until both are soft, about 5 minutes. Add the tomato paste, garlic, and oregano and cook 2 minutes, stirring constantly.
2. Stir in the water and lentils. Bring to a boil, then reduce the heat to medium-low and cook for 5 minutes, covered.
3. Add the tomatoes (and juice if using diced) and vinegar. Replace the lid, reduce the heat to low and cook until the lentils are tender, about 30 minutes.
4. Remove the sauce from the heat and season with salt and pepper to taste. Garnish with the basil and serve over the cooked pasta.

Nutrition Info:

- Per Serving: Calories: 463;Fat: 15.9g;Protein: 12.5g;Carbs: 70.8g.

Spinach Farfalle With Ricotta Cheese

Servings:4
Cooking Time:25 Minutes
Ingredients:

- ¼ cup extra-virgin olive oil
- ½ cup crumbled ricotta cheese
- 2 tbsp black olives, halved
- 4 cups fresh baby spinach, chopped
- 2 tbsp scallions, chopped
- 16 oz farfalle pasta
- ¼ cup red wine vinegar
- 2 tsp lemon juice
- Salt and black pepper to taste

Directions:

1. Cook the farfalle pasta to pack instructions, drain and let it to cool. Mix the scallions, spinach, and cooled pasta in a bowl. Top with ricotta and olives. Combine the vinegar, olive oil, lemon juice, salt, and pepper in another bowl. Pour over the pasta mixture and toss to combine. Serve chilled.

Nutrition Info:

- Per Serving: Calories: 377;Fat: 16g;Protein: 12g;Carbs: 44g.

Bell Pepper & Bean Salad

Servings:6
Cooking Time:30 Minutes
Ingredients:

- ¼ cup extra-virgin olive oil
- 3 garlic cloves, minced
- 2 cans cannellini beans
- Salt and black pepper to taste
- 2 tsp sherry vinegar
- 1 red onion, sliced
- 1 red bell pepper, chopped
- ¼ cup chopped fresh parsley
- 2 tsp chopped fresh chives
- ¼ tsp crushed red pepper

Directions:

1. Warm 1 tbsp of olive oil in a saucepan over medium heat. Sauté the garlic until it turns golden but not brown, about 3 minutes. Add beans, 2 cups of water, and salt, and pepper, and bring to a simmer. Heat off. Let sit for 20 minutes.
2. Mix well the vinegar and red onion in a salad bowl. Drain the beans and remove the garlic. Add beans, remaining olive oil, bell pepper, parsley, crushed red pepper, chives, salt, and pepper to the onion mixture and gently toss to combine.

Nutrition Info:

- Per Serving: Calories: 131;Fat: 7.7g;Protein: 6g;Carbs: 13.5g.

Spinach Lentils

Servings:6
Cooking Time:30 Minutes
Ingredients:
- 2 tbsp olive oil
- 4 garlic cloves, sliced thin
- Salt and black pepper to taste
- 1 onion, chopped
- 1 tsp ground coriander
- 1 tsp dried thyme
- 1 tsp ground cumin
- 1 cup lentils, rinsed
- 8 oz spinach, chopped

Directions:
1. Warm the olive oil in a pot over medium heat. Sauté the garlic for 2-3 minutes, stirring often, until crisp and golden but not brown. Remove the garlic to a paper towel–lined plate and season lightly with salt; set aside. Add the onion to the pot and cook for 3 minutes until softened and lightly browned. Stir in salt, thyme, coriander, and cumin for 1 minute until fragrant.
2. Pour in 2 ½ cups of water and lentils and bring to a simmer. Lower the heat to low, cover, and simmer gently, stirring occasionally for 15 minutes until lentils are mostly tender but still intact. Stir in spinach and cook until spinach is wilted, about 5 minutes. Adjust the taste with salt and pepper. Sprinkle with toasted garlic and serve warm.

Nutrition Info:
- Per Serving: Calories: 189;Fat: 5.5g;Protein: 9g;Carbs: 27.1g.

Curry Apple Couscous With Leeks And Pecans

Servings:4
Cooking Time: 8 Minutes
Ingredients:
- 2 teaspoons extra-virgin olive oil
- 2 leeks, white parts only, sliced
- 1 apple, diced
- 2 cups cooked couscous
- 2 tablespoons curry powder
- ½ cup chopped pecans

Directions:
1. Heat the olive oil in a skillet over medium heat until shimmering.
2. Add the leeks and sauté for 5 minutes or until soft.
3. Add the diced apple and cook for 3 more minutes until tender.
4. Add the couscous and curry powder. Stir to combine.

5. Transfer them in a large serving bowl, then mix in the pecans and serve.
Nutrition Info:
- Per Serving: Calories: 254;Fat: 11.9g;Protein: 5.4g;Carbs: 34.3g.

Basic Brown Rice Pilaf With Capers

Servings:4
Cooking Time:30 Minutes
Ingredients:
- 2 tbsp olive oil
- 1 cup brown rice
- 1 onion, chopped
- 1 celery stalk, chopped
- 2 garlic cloves, minced
- ½ cup capers, rinsed
- Salt and black pepper to taste
- 2 tbsp parsley, chopped

Directions:
1. Warm the olive oil in a skillet over medium heat. Sauté celery, garlic, and onion for 10 minutes. Stir in rice, capers, 2 cups of water, salt, and pepper and cook for 25 minutes. Serve topped with parsley.

Nutrition Info:
- Per Serving: Calories: 230;Fat: 8.9g;Protein: 7g;Carbs: 16g.

Marrakech-style Couscous

Servings:4
Cooking Time:25 Minutes
Ingredients:
- 2 tbsp olive oil
- 1 cup instant couscous
- 2 tbsp dried apricots, chopped
- 2 tbsp dried sultanas
- ½ onion, minced
- 1 orange, juiced and zested
- ¼ tsp paprika
- ¼ tsp turmeric
- ½ tsp garlic powder
- ½ tsp ground cumin
- ¼ tsp ground cinnamon
- Salt and black pepper to taste

Directions:
1. Warm olive oil in a pot over medium heat and sauté onion for 3 minutes. Add in orange juice, orange zest, garlic powder, cumin, salt, paprika, turmeric, cinnamon, black pepper, and 2 cups of water and bring to a boil. Stir in apricots, couscous, and sultanas. Remove from the heat and let sit covered for 5 minutes. Fluff the couscous using a fork. Serve.

Nutrition Info:

- Per Serving: Calories: 246;Fat: 7.4g;Protein: 5g;Carbs: 41.8g.

Kale Chicken With Pappardelle

Servings:4
Cooking Time:30 Min + Chilling Time
Ingredients:

- 1 cup grated Parmigiano-Reggiano cheese
- 4 chicken thighs, cut into 1-inch pieces
- 3 tbsp olive oil
- 16 oz pappardelle pasta
- Salt and black pepper to taste
- 1 yellow onion, chopped
- 4 garlic cloves, minced
- 12 cherry tomatoes, halved
- ½ cup chicken broth
- 2 cups baby kale, chopped
- 2 tbsp pine nuts for topping

Directions:

1. In a pot of boiling water, cook the pappardelle pasta for 8-10 minutes until al dente. Drain and set aside.
2. Heat the olive oil in a medium pot. Season the chicken with salt and pepper and sear in the oil until golden brown on the outside. Transfer to a plate and set aside. Add the onion and garlic to the oil and cook until softened and fragrant, 3 minutes. Mix in tomatoes and chicken broth and cook over low heat until the tomatoes soften and the liquid reduces by half. Season with salt and pepper. Return the chicken to the pot and stir in kale. Allow wilting for 2 minutes. Spoon the pappardelle onto serving plates, top with kale sauce and Parmigianino-Reggiano cheese. Garnish with pine nuts.

Nutrition Info:

- Per Serving: Calories: 740;Fat: 53g;Protein: 50g;Carbs: 15g.

Mashed Beans With Cumin

Servings:4
Cooking Time: 10 To 12 Minutes
Ingredients:

- 1 tablespoon extra-virgin olive oil, plus extra for serving
- 4 garlic cloves, minced
- 1 teaspoon ground cumin
- 2 cans fava beans
- 3 tablespoons tahini
- 2 tablespoons lemon juice, plus lemon wedges for serving
- Salt and pepper, to taste
- 1 tomato, cored and cut into ½-inch pieces
- 1 small onion, chopped finely
- 2 hard-cooked large eggs, chopped
- 2 tablespoons minced fresh parsley

Directions:

1. Add the olive oil, garlic and cumin to a medium saucepan over medium heat. Cook for about 2 minutes, or until fragrant.
2. Stir in the beans with their liquid and tahini. Bring to a simmer and cook for 8 to 10 minutes, or until the liquid thickens slightly.
3. Turn off the heat, mash the beans to a coarse consistency with a potato masher. Stir in the lemon juice and 1 teaspoon pepper. Season with salt and pepper.
4. Transfer the mashed beans to a serving dish. Top with the tomato, onion, eggs and parsley. Drizzle with the extra olive oil.
5. Serve with the lemon wedges.

Nutrition Info:

- Per Serving: Calories: 125;Fat: 8.6g;Protein: 4.9g;Carbs: 9.1g.

Mustard Vegetable Millet

Servings:6
Cooking Time:35 Minutes
Ingredients:

- 6 oz okra, cut into 1-inch lengths
- 3 tbsp olive oil
- 6 oz asparagus, chopped
- Salt and black pepper to taste
- 1 ½ cups whole millet
- 2 tbsp lemon juice
- 2 tbsp minced shallot
- 1 tsp Dijon mustard
- 6 oz cherry tomatoes, halved
- 3 tbsp chopped fresh dill
- 2 oz goat cheese, crumbled

Directions:

1. In a large pot, bring 4 quarts of water to a boil. Add asparagus, snap peas, and salt and cook until crisp-tender, about 3 minutes. Using a slotted spoon, transfer vegetables to a large plate and let cool completely, about 15 minutes. Add millet to water, return to a boil, and cook until grains are tender, 15-20 minutes.
2. Drain millet, spread in rimmed baking sheet, and let cool completely, 15 minutes. Whisk oil, lemon juice, shallot, mustard, salt, and pepper in a large bowl. Add vegetables, millet, tomatoes, dill, and half of the goat cheese and toss gently to combine. Season with salt and pepper. Sprinkle with remaining goat cheese to serve.

Nutrition Info:

- Per Serving: Calories: 315;Fat: 19g;Protein: 13g;Carbs: 35g.

Caprese Pasta With Roasted Asparagus

Servings:6
Cooking Time: 25 Minutes
Ingredients:
- 8 ounces uncooked small pasta, like orecchiette (little ears) or farfalle (bow ties)
- 1½ pounds fresh asparagus, ends trimmed and stalks chopped into 1-inch pieces
- 1½ cups grape tomatoes, halved
- 2 tablespoons extra-virgin olive oil
- ¼ teaspoon kosher salt
- ¼ teaspoon freshly ground black pepper
- 2 cups fresh Mozzarella, drained and cut into bite-size pieces
- ⅓ cup torn fresh basil leaves
- 2 tablespoons balsamic vinegar

Directions:
1. Preheat the oven to 400ºF.
2. In a large stockpot of salted water, cook the pasta for about 8 to 10 minutes. Drain and reserve about ¼ cup of the cooking liquid.
3. Meanwhile, in a large bowl, toss together the asparagus, tomatoes, oil, salt and pepper. Spread the mixture onto a large, rimmed baking sheet and bake in the oven for 15 minutes, stirring twice during cooking.
4. Remove the vegetables from the oven and add the cooked pasta to the baking sheet. Mix with a few tablespoons of cooking liquid to help the sauce become smoother and the saucy vegetables stick to the pasta.
5. Gently mix in the Mozzarella and basil. Drizzle with the balsamic vinegar. Serve from the baking sheet or pour the pasta into a large bowl.

Nutrition Info:
- Per Serving: Calories: 147;Fat: 3.0g;Protein: 16.0g;Carbs: 17.0g.

Rice And Blueberry Stuffed Sweet Potatoes

Servings:4
Cooking Time: 20 Minutes
Ingredients:
- 2 cups cooked wild rice
- ½ cup dried blueberries
- ½ cup chopped hazelnuts
- ½ cup shredded Swiss chard
- 1 teaspoon chopped fresh thyme
- 1 scallion, white and green parts, peeled and thinly sliced
- Sea salt and freshly ground black pepper, to taste
- 4 sweet potatoes, baked in the skin until tender

Directions:

1. Preheat the oven to 400ºF.
2. Combine all the ingredients, except for the sweet potatoes, in a large bowl. Stir to mix well.
3. Cut the top third of the sweet potato off length wire, then scoop most of the sweet potato flesh out.
4. Fill the potato with the wild rice mixture, then set the sweet potato on a greased baking sheet.
5. Bake in the preheated oven for 20 minutes or until the sweet potato skin is lightly charred.
6. Serve immediately.

Nutrition Info:
- Per Serving: Calories: 393;Fat: 7.1g;Protein: 10.2g;Carbs: 76.9g.

Garlic And Parsley Chickpeas

Servings:4
Cooking Time: 18 To 20 Minutes
Ingredients:
- ¼ cup extra-virgin olive oil, divided
- 4 garlic cloves, sliced thinly
- ⅛ teaspoon red pepper flakes
- 1 onion, chopped finely
- ¼ teaspoon salt, plus more to taste
- Black pepper, to taste
- 2 cans chickpeas, rinsed
- 1 cup vegetable broth
- 2 tablespoons minced fresh parsley
- 2 teaspoons lemon juice

Directions:
1. Add 3 tablespoons of the olive oil, garlic, and pepper flakes to a skillet over medium heat. Cook for about 3 minutes, stirring constantly, or until the garlic turns golden but not brown.
2. Stir in the onion and ¼ teaspoon salt and cook for 5 to 7 minutes, or until softened and lightly browned.
3. Add the chickpeas and broth to the skillet and bring to a simmer. Reduce the heat to medium-low, cover, and cook for about 7 minutes, or until the chickpeas are cooked through and flavors meld.
4. Uncover, increase the heat to high and continue to cook for about 3 minutes more, or until nearly all liquid has evaporated.
5. Turn off the heat, stir in the parsley and lemon juice. Season to taste with salt and pepper and drizzle with remaining 1 tablespoon of the olive oil.
6. Serve warm.

Nutrition Info:
- Per Serving: Calories: 220;Fat: 11.4g;Protein: 6.5g;Carbs: 24.6g.

Quinoa & Watercress Salad With Nuts

Servings:4
Cooking Time:5 Minutes
Ingredients:
- 2 boiled eggs, cut into wedges
- 2 cups watercress
- 2 cups cherry tomatoes, halved
- 1 cucumber, sliced
- 1 cup quinoa, cooked
- 1 cup almonds, chopped
- 2 tbsp olive oil
- 1 avocado, peeled and sliced
- 2 tbsp fresh cilantro, chopped
- Salt to taste
- 1 lemon, juiced

Directions:
1. Place watercress, cherry tomatoes, cucumber, quinoa, almonds, olive oil, cilantro, salt, and lemon juice in a bowl and toss to combine. Top with egg wedges and avocado slices and serve immediately.

Nutrition Info:
- Per Serving: Calories: 530;Fat: 35g;Protein: 20g;Carbs: 45g.

Baked Rolled Oat With Pears And Pecans

Servings:6
Cooking Time: 30 Minutes
Ingredients:
- 2 tablespoons coconut oil, melted, plus more for greasing the pan
- 3 ripe pears, cored and diced
- 2 cups unsweetened almond milk
- 1 tablespoon pure vanilla extract
- ¼ cup pure maple syrup
- 2 cups gluten-free rolled oats
- ½ cup raisins
- ¾ cup chopped pecans
- ¼ teaspoon ground nutmeg
- 1 teaspoon ground cinnamon
- ½ teaspoon ground ginger
- ¼ teaspoon sea salt

Directions:
1. Preheat the oven to 350ºF. Grease a baking dish with melted coconut oil, then spread the pears in a single layer on the baking dish evenly.
2. Combine the almond milk, vanilla extract, maple syrup, and coconut oil in a bowl. Stir to mix well.

3. Combine the remaining ingredients in a separate large bowl. Stir to mix well. Fold the almond milk mixture in the bowl, then pour the mixture over the pears.
4. Place the baking dish in the preheated oven and bake for 30 minutes or until lightly browned and set.
5. Serve immediately.

Nutrition Info:
- Per Serving: Calories: 479;Fat: 34.9g;Protein: 8.8g;Carbs: 50.1g.

Autumn Vegetable & Rigatoni Bake

Servings:6
Cooking Time:45 Minutes
Ingredients:
- 2 tbsp grated Pecorino-Romano cheese
- 2 tbsp olive oil
- 1 lb pumpkin, chopped
- 1 zucchini, chopped
- 1 onion, chopped
- 1 lb rigatoni
- Salt and black pepper to taste
- ½ tsp garlic powder
- ½ cup dry white wine

Directions:
1. Preheat oven to 420 F. Combine zucchini, pumpkin, onion, and olive oil in a bowl. Arrange on a lined aluminum foil sheet and season with salt, pepper, and garlic powder. Bake for 30 minutes until tender. In a pot of boiling water, cook rigatoni for 8-10 minutes until al dente. Drain and set aside.
2. In a food processor, place ½ cup of the roasted veggies and wine and pulse until smooth. Transfer to a skillet over medium heat. Stir in rigatoni and cook until heated through. Top with the remaining vegetables and Pecorino cheese to serve.

Nutrition Info:
- Per Serving: Calories: 186;Fat: 11g;Protein: 10g;Carbs: 15g.

Easy Bulgur Tabbouleh

Servings:4
Cooking Time:30 Minutes
Ingredients:
- 1 cucumber, peeled and chopped
- ¼ cup extra-virgin olive oil
- 8 cherry tomatoes, quartered
- 1 cup bulgur, rinsed
- 4 scallions, chopped
- ½ cup fresh parsley, chopped
- 1 lemon, juiced
- Salt and black pepper to taste

Directions:

1. Place the bulgur in a large pot with plenty of salted water, cover, and boil for 13-15 minutes. Drain and let it cool completely. Add scallions, tomatoes, cucumber, and parsley to the cooled bulgur and mix to combine. In another bowl, whisk the lemon juice, olive oil, salt, and pepper. Pour the dressing over the bulgur mixture and toss to combine. Serve.

Nutrition Info:

- Per Serving: Calories: 291;Fat: 13.7g;Protein: 7g;Carbs: 40g.

Bolognese Penne Bake

Servings:6
Cooking Time:55 Minutes
Ingredients:

- 1 lb penne pasta
- 1 lb ground beef
- A pinch of two salt
- 1 basil-tomato sauce
- 1 lb baby spinach, washed
- 3 cups mozzarella, shredded

Directions:

1. Bring a pot of salted water to a boil, add the pasta, and cook until al dente. Reserve 1 cup of the pasta water; drain the pasta.
2. Preheat the oven to 350F. In a skillet over medium heat, stir-fry the ground beef along with a pinch of salt until browned, 5 minutes. Stir in basil-tomato sauce and 2 cups of pasta water and let simmer for 5 minutes. Add a handful of spinach, one at a time, into the sauce, and cook for 3 minutes.
3. In a large baking dish, add the pasta and pour the sauce over it. Stir in 1 ½ cups of mozzarella cheese, cover the dish with aluminum foil and bake for 20 minutes. After 20 minutes, remove the foil, top with the remaining mozzarella, and bake for another 8-12 minutes until golden brown. Serve.

Nutrition Info:

- Per Serving: Calories: 445;Fat: 21g;Protein: 29g;Carbs: 43g.

Lemony Green Quinoa

Servings:4
Cooking Time:30 Minutes
Ingredients:

- 2 tbsp olive oil
- 1 onion, chopped
- 2 garlic cloves, minced
- 1 cup quinoa, rinsed
- 1 lb asparagus, chopped
- 2 tbsp fresh parsley, chopped
- 2 tbsp lemon juice
- 1 tsp lemon zest, grated
- ½ lb green beans, trimmed and halved
- Salt and black pepper to taste

- ½ lb cherry tomatoes, halved

Directions:

1. Heat olive oil in a pot over medium heat and sauté onion and garlic for 3 minutes until soft. Stir in quinoa for 1-2 minutes. Pour in 2 cups of water and season with salt and pepper. Bring to a bowl and reduce the heat. Simmer for 5 minutes. Stir in green beans and asparagus and cook for another 10 minutes. Remove from the heat and mix in cherry tomatoes, lemon juice and lemon zest. Top with parsley and serve.

Nutrition Info:

- Per Serving: Calories: 430;Fat: 16g;Protein: 17g;Carbs: 60g.

Rice & Lentil Salad With Caramelized Onions

Servings:4
Cooking Time:1 Hour 15 Minutes
Ingredients:

- ¼ cup olive oil
- 2 cups lentils
- 1 cup brown rice
- 4 ½ cups water
- ½ tsp dried thyme
- ½ tsp dried tarragon
- 3 onions, peeled and sliced
- Salt and black pepper to taste

Directions:

1. Place the lentils and rice in a large saucepan with water. Bring to a boil, cover, and simmer for 23 minutes or until almost tender. Stir in the seasonings and cook for 25-30 minutes or until the rice is tender and the water is absorbed.
2. In a separate saucepan, warm the olive oil over medium heat. Add the onions and cook slowly, stirring frequently, until the onions brown and caramelize, for 17-20 minutes. Top with the caramelized onions. Serve and enjoy!

Nutrition Info:

- Per Serving: Calories: 498;Fat: 19g;Protein: 15g;Carbs: 63g.

Mozzarella & Asparagus Pasta

Servings:6
Cooking Time:40 Minutes
Ingredients:

- 1 ½ lb asparagus, trimmed, cut into 1-inch
- 2 tbsp olive oil
- 8 oz orecchiette
- 2 cups cherry tomatoes, halved
- Salt and black pepper to taste
- 2 cups fresh mozzarella, drained and chopped
- ⅓ cup torn basil leaves
- 2 tbsp balsamic vinegar

Directions:

1. Preheat oven to 390 F. In a large pot, cook the pasta according to the directions. Drain, reserving ¼ cup of cooking water.

2. In the meantime, in a large bowl, toss in asparagus, cherry tomatoes, oil, pepper, and salt. Spread the mixture onto a rimmed baking sheet and bake for 15 minutes, stirring twice throughout cooking. Remove the veggies from the oven, and add the cooked pasta to the baking sheet. Mix with a few tbsp of pasta water to smooth the sauce and veggies. Slowly mix in the mozzarella and basil. Drizzle with the balsamic vinegar and serve in bowls.

Nutrition Info:

- Per Serving: Calories: 188;Fat: 11g;Protein: 14g;Carbs: 23g.

Linguine A La Carbonara

Servings:4
Cooking Time:30 Minutes
Ingredients:

- 1 ¼ cups heavy whipping cream
- 16 oz linguine
- 4 bacon slices, chopped
- ¼ cup mayonnaise
- Salt and black pepper to taste
- 4 egg yolks
- 1 cup grated Parmesan cheese

Directions:

1. In a pot of boiling water, cook the linguine pasta for 8-10 minutes until al dente. Drain and set aside.

2. Add the bacon to a skillet and cook over medium heat until crispy, 5 minutes. Set aside. Pour heavy cream into a pot and allow simmering for 5 minutes. Whisk in mayonnaise and season with salt and pepper. Cook for 1 minute and spoon 2 tablespoons of the mixture into a medium bowl. Allow cooling and mix in the egg yolks. Pour the mixture into the pot and mix quickly. Stir in Parmesan cheese and fold in the pasta. Cook for 1 minute until the pasta is heated through.

Nutrition Info:

- Per Serving: Calories: 470;Fat: 36g;Protein: 25g;Carbs: 9g.

Easy Simple Pesto Pasta

Servings:4
Cooking Time: 8 Minutes
Ingredients:

- 1 pound spaghetti
- 4 cups fresh basil leaves, stems removed
- 3 cloves garlic
- 1 teaspoon salt
- ½ teaspoon freshly ground black pepper
- ½ cup toasted pine nuts
- ¼ cup lemon juice
- ½ cup grated Parmesan cheese

- 1 cup extra-virgin olive oil

Directions:

1. Bring a large pot of salted water to a boil. Add the spaghetti to the pot and cook for 8 minutes.

2. In a food processor, place the remaining ingredients, except for the olive oil, and pulse.

3. While the processor is running, slowly drizzle the olive oil through the top opening. Process until all the olive oil has been added.

4. Reserve ½ cup of the cooking liquid. Drain the pasta and put it into a large bowl. Add the pesto and cooking liquid to the bowl of pasta and toss everything together.

5. Serve immediately.

Nutrition Info:

- Per Serving: Calories: 1067;Fat: 72.0g;Protein: 23.0g;Carbs: 91g.

Bulgur Pilaf With Kale And Tomatoes

Servings:2
Cooking Time: 10 Minutes
Ingredients:

- 2 tablespoons olive oil
- 2 cloves garlic, minced
- 1 bunch kale, trimmed and cut into bite-sized pieces
- Juice of 1 lemon
- 2 cups cooked bulgur wheat
- 1 pint cherry tomatoes, halved
- Sea salt and freshly ground pepper, to taste

Directions:

1. Heat the olive oil in a large skillet over medium heat. Add the garlic and sauté for 1 minute.

2. Add the kale leaves and stir to coat. Cook for 5 minutes until leaves are cooked through and thoroughly wilted.

3. Add the lemon juice, bulgur and tomatoes. Season with sea salt and freshly ground pepper to taste, then serve.

Nutrition Info:

- Per Serving: Calories: 300;Fat: 14.0g;Protein: 6.2g;Carbs: 37.8g.

Raspberry & Nut Quinoa

Servings:4
Cooking Time:5 Minutes
Ingredients:

- 1 tbsp honey
- 2 cups almond milk
- 2 cups quinoa, cooked
- ½ tsp cinnamon powder
- 1 cup raspberries
- ¼ cup walnuts, chopped

Directions:

1. Combine quinoa, milk, cinnamon powder, honey, raspberries, and walnuts in a bowl. Serve in individual bowls.

Mediterranean-style Beans And Greens

Servings:2
Cooking Time: 15 Minutes
Ingredients:
- 1 can diced tomatoes with juice
- 1 can cannellini beans, drained and rinsed
- 2 tablespoons chopped green olives, plus 1 or 2 sliced for garnish
- ¼ cup vegetable broth, plus more as needed
- 1 teaspoon extra-virgin olive oil
- 2 cloves garlic, minced
- 4 cups arugula
- ¼ cup freshly squeezed lemon juice

Directions:
1. In a medium saucepan, bring the tomatoes, beans and chopped olives to a low boil, adding just enough broth to make the ingredients saucy (you may need more than ¼ cup if your canned tomatoes don't have a lot of juice). Reduce heat to low and simmer for about 5 minutes.
2. Meanwhile, in a large skillet, heat the olive oil over medium-high heat. When the oil is hot and starts to shimmer, add garlic and sauté just until it starts to turn slightly tan, about 30 seconds. Add the arugula and lemon juice, stirring to coat leaves with the olive oil and juice. Cover and reduce heat to low. Simmer for 3 to 5 minutes.
3. Serve beans over the greens and garnish with olive slices.

Nutrition Info:
- Per Serving: Calories: 262;Fat: 5.9g;Protein: 13.2g;Carbs: 40.4g.

Tomato Sauce And Basil Pesto Fettuccine

Servings:4
Cooking Time: 15 Minutes
Ingredients:
- 4 Roma tomatoes, diced
- 2 teaspoons no-salt-added tomato paste
- 1 tablespoon chopped fresh oregano
- 2 garlic cloves, minced
- 1 cup low-sodium vegetable soup
- ½ teaspoon sea salt
- 1 packed cup fresh basil leaves
- ¼ cup pine nuts
- ¼ cup grated Parmesan cheese
- 2 tablespoons extra-virgin olive oil
- 1 pound cooked whole-grain fettuccine

Directions:
1. Put the tomatoes, tomato paste, oregano, garlic, vegetable soup, and salt in a skillet. Stir to mix well.
2. Cook over medium heat for 10 minutes or until lightly thickened.
3. Put the remaining ingredients, except for the fettuccine, in a food processor and pulse to combine until smooth.
4. Pour the puréed basil mixture into the tomato mixture, then add the fettuccine. Cook for a few minutes or until heated through and the fettuccine is well coated.
5. Serve immediately.

Nutrition Info:
- Per Serving: Calories: 389;Fat: 22.7g;Protein: 9.7g;Carbs: 40.2g.

Hummus & Bean Lettuce Rolls

Servings:4
Cooking Time:20 Minutes
Ingredients:
- 2 tbsp extra-virgin olive oil
- ½ cup diced red onion
- 2 chopped fresh tomatoes
- 1 tsp paprika
- ¼ tsp ground nutmeg
- Salt and black pepper to taste
- 1 can cannellini beans
- ¼ cup chopped fresh parsley
- ½ cup hummus
- 8 romaine lettuce leaves

Directions:
1. Warm the olive oil in a skillet over medium heat. Add the onion and cook for 3 minutes, stirring occasionally. Add the tomatoes and paprika and cook for 3 more minutes, stirring occasionally. Add the beans and cook for 3 more minutes, stirring occasionally. Remove from the heat and sprinkle with salt, pepper, cumin, nutmeg, and parsley. Stir well.
2. Spread the hummus on the lettuce leaves. Spoon the warm bean mixture down the center of each leaf. Fold one side of the lettuce leaf over the filling lengthwise, then fold over the other side to make a wrap and serve.

Nutrition Info:
- Per Serving: Calories: 188;Fat: 5g;Protein: 10g;Carbs: 28g.

Minty Lamb Risotto

Servings:4
Cooking Time:90 Minutes
Ingredients:

- 2 tbsp olive oil
- 2 garlic cloves, minced
- 1 onion, chopped
- 1 lb lamb, cubed
- Salt and black pepper to taste
- 2 cups vegetable stock
- 1 cup arborio rice
- 2 tbsp mint, chopped
- 1 cup Parmesan, grated

Directions:

1. Warm the olive oil in a skillet over medium heat and cook the onion for 5 minutes. Put in lamb and cook for another 5 minutes. Stir in garlic, salt, pepper, and stock and bring to a simmer; cook for 1 hour. Stir in rice and cook for 18-20 minutes. Top with Parmesan cheese and mint and serve.

Nutrition Info:

- Per Serving: Calories: 310;Fat: 14g;Protein: 15g;Carbs: 17g.

Creamy Mussel Spaghetti

Servings:4
Cooking Time:20 Minutes
Ingredients:

- 1 lb mussels, debearded and rinsed
- 2 tbsp olive oil
- 16 oz spaghetti, broken in half
- 1 cup white wine
- 3 shallots, finely chopped
- 6 garlic cloves, minced
- 2 tsp red chili flakes
- ½ cup fish stock
- 1 ½ cups heavy cream
- 2 tbsp chopped fresh parsley
- Salt and black pepper to taste

Directions:

1. Boil water in a pot over medium heat and place in the pasta. Cook for 8-10 minutes for al dente. Drain and set aside.

2. Pour mussels and white wine into a pot, cover, and cook for 4 minutes. Occasionally stir until the mussels have opened. Strain the mussels and reserve the cooking liquid. Allow cooling, discard any mussels with closed shells, and remove the meat out of ¾ of the mussel shells. Set aside the remaining mussels in the shells.

3. Heat olive oil in a skillet and sauté shallots, garlic, and chili flakes for 3 minutes. Mix in reduced wine and fish stock. Allow boiling and whisk in the heavy cream. Taste the sauce and adjust the seasoning with salt and pepper; top with parsley. Pour in the pasta, mussels and toss well in the sauce.

Nutrition Info:

- Per Serving: Calories: 471;Fat: 34g;Protein: 19g;Carbs: 19g.

Genovese Mussel Linguine

Servings:4
Cooking Time:40 Minutes
Ingredients:

- 1 lb mussels, scrubbed and debearded
- 1 tbsp olive oil
- ½ cup Pinot Grigio wine
- 2 garlic cloves, minced
- ½ tsp red pepper flakes
- ½ lemon, zested and juiced
- 1 lb linguine
- Salt and black pepper to taste
- 2 tbsp parsley, finely chopped

Directions:

1. In a saucepan, bring mussels and wine to a boil, cover, and cook, shaking pan occasionally, until mussels open, 5-7 minutes. As they open, remove them with a slotted spoon into a bowl. Discard all closed mussels. Drain steaming liquid through fine-mesh strainer into a bowl, avoiding any gritty sediment that has settled on the bottom of the pan.

2. Wipe the pan clean. Warm the olive oil in the pan and stir-fry garlic and pepper flake until the garlic turn golden, 3 minutes. Stir in reserved mussel liquid and lemon zest and juice, bring to a simmer and cook for 3-4 minutes. Stir in mussels and cook until heated through, 3 minutes.

3. Bring a large pot filled with salted water to a boil. Add pasta and cook until al dente. Reserve ½ cup of cooking liquid, drain pasta and return it to pot. Add the sauce and parsley and toss to combine and season to taste. Adjust consistency with the reserved cooking liquid as needed and serve.

Nutrition Info:

- Per Serving: Calories: 423;Fat: 9g;Protein: 16g;Carbs: 37g.

Simple Green Rice

Servings:4
Cooking Time:35 Minutes
Ingredients:
- 2 tbsp butter
- 4 spring onions, sliced
- 1 leek, sliced
- 1 medium zucchini, chopped
- 5 oz broccoli florets
- 2 oz curly kale
- ½ cup frozen green peas
- 2 cloves garlic, minced
- 1 thyme sprig, chopped
- 1 rosemary sprig, chopped
- 1 cup white rice
- 2 cups vegetable broth
- 1 large tomato, chopped
- 2 oz Kalamata olives, sliced

Directions:
1. Melt the butter in a saucepan over medium heat. Cook the spring onions, leek, and zucchini for about 4-5 minutes or until tender. Add in the garlic, thyme, and rosemary and continue to sauté for about 1 minute or until aromatic. Add in the rice, broth, and tomato. Bring to a boil, turn the heat to a gentle simmer, and cook for about 10-12 minutes. Stir in broccoli, kale, and green peas, and continue cooking for 5 minutes. Fluff the rice with a fork and garnish with olives.

Nutrition Info:
- Per Serving: Calories: 403;Fat: 11g;Protein: 9g;Carbs: 64g.

Sides , Salads, And Soups Recipes

Mushroom Sauce

Servings:4
Cooking Time:15 Minutes
Ingredients:
- 1 cup cremini mushrooms, chopped
- 2 tbsp olive oil
- 1 small onion, chopped
- 2 garlic cloves, minced
- 3 tbsp butter
- ½ cup white wine
- ½ cup vegetable broth
- 1 cup heavy cream
- 2 tbsp parsley, chopped

Directions:
1. Heat the olive oil in a pan over medium. Add the onion and garlic and sauté until the onion is translucent, 3 minutes. Add the butter and mushrooms and cook for 5-7 minutes until the mushrooms are tender. Pour in the wine and scrape up any browned bits from the bottom of the pan. Simmer for 3-4 minutes. Add the vegetable broth and simmer for 5 minutes until the sauce reduces by about three quarters. Add the heavy cream and simmer for 2-3 minutes. Sprinkle with parsley. Serve and enjoy!

Nutrition Info:
- Per Serving: Calories: 283;Fat: 27g;Protein: 2.1g;Carbs: 5g.

Party Summer Salad

Servings:4
Cooking Time:10 Minutes
Ingredients:
- ½ cup extra virgin olive oil
- 2 cucumbers, sliced
- 2 mixed bell peppers, sliced
- 2 tomatoes, sliced
- 2 green onions, thinly sliced
- 2 gem lettuces, sliced
- 1 cup arugula
- 2 tbsp parsley, chopped
- Salt to taste
- 1 cup feta cheese, crumbled
- 3 tbsp lemon juice

Directions:
1. In a bowl, mix the cucumbers, bell peppers, green onions, gem lettuce, and arugula. In a small bowl, whisk the olive oil, lemon juice, and salt. Pour over the salad and toss to coat. Scatter the feta over and top with tomato and parsley.

Nutrition Info:
- Per Serving: Calories: 398;Fat: 34g;Protein: 19g;Carbs: 20g.

Chorizo & Fire-roasted Tomato Soup

Servings:4
Cooking Time:25 Minutes
Ingredients:
- 28 oz fire-roasted diced tomatoes
- 1 tbsp olive oil
- 2 shallots, chopped
- 3 cloves garlic, minced
- Salt and black pepper to taste
- 4 cups beef broth
- ½ cup fresh ripe tomatoes
- 1 tbsp red wine vinegar
- 3 chorizo sausage, chopped
- ½ cup thinly chopped basil

Directions:
1. Warm the olive oil on Sauté in your Instant Pot. Cook the chorizo until crispy, stirring occasionally, about 5 minutes. Remove to a plate. Add the garlic and shallots to the pot and sauté for 3 minutes until soft. Season with salt and pepper.
2. Stir in red wine vinegar, broth, diced tomatoes, and ripe tomatoes. Seal the lid and cook on High Pressure for 8 minutes. Release the pressure quickly. Pour the soup into a blender and process until smooth. Divide into bowls, top with chorizo, and decorate with basil.

Nutrition Info:
- Per Serving: Calories: 771;Fat: 27g;Protein: 40g;Carbs: 117g.

Bell Pepper & Shrimp Salad With Avocado

Servings:4
Cooking Time:10 Min + Cooling Time
Ingredients:
- 1 lb shrimp, peeled and deveined
- 2 tbsp olive oil
- 1 tbsp lemon juice
- 1 yellow bell pepper, sliced
- 1 Romano lettuce, torn
- 1 avocado, chopped
- Salt to taste
- 12 cherry tomatoes, halved

Directions:
1. Preheat grill pan over high heat. Drizzle the shrimp with some olive oil and arrange them on the preheated grill pan. Sear for 5 minutes on both sides until pink and cooked through. Let cool completely.
2. In a serving plate, arrange the lettuce, and top with bell pepper, shrimp, avocado, and cherry tomatoes. In a bowl, add the lemon juice, salt, and olive oil and whisk to combine. Drizzle the dressing over the salad and serve immediately.

Nutrition Info:
- Per Serving: Calories: 380;Fat: 24g;Protein: 25g;Carbs: 23g.

Cheese & Broccoli Quiche

Servings:4
Cooking Time:45 Minutes
Ingredients:
- 1 tsp Mediterranean seasoning
- 3 eggs
- ½ cup heavy cream
- 3 tbsp olive oil
- 1 red onion, chopped
- 2 garlic cloves, minced
- 2 oz mozzarella, shredded
- 1 lb broccoli, cut into florets

Directions:
1. Preheat oven to 320 F. Warm the oil in a pan over medium heat. Sauté the onion and garlic until just tender and fragrant. Add in the broccoli and continue to cook until crisp-tender for about 4 minutes. Spoon the mixture into a greased casserole dish. Beat the eggs with heavy cream and Mediterranean seasoning. Spoon this mixture over the broccoli layer. Bake for 18-20 minutes. Top with the shredded cheese and broil for 5 to 6 minutes or until hot and bubbly on the top. Serve.

Nutrition Info:
- Per Serving: Calories: 198;Fat: 14g;Protein: 5g;Carbs: 12g.

Mediterranean Tomato Hummus Soup

Servings:2
Cooking Time: 10 Minutes
Ingredients:
- 1 can crushed tomatoes with basil
- 2 cups low-sodium chicken stock
- 1 cup roasted red pepper hummus
- Salt, to taste
- ¼ cup thinly sliced fresh basil leaves, for garnish (optional)

Directions:
1. Combine the canned tomatoes, hummus, and chicken stock in a blender and blend until smooth. Pour the mixture into a saucepan and bring it to a boil. Season with salt to taste.
2. Serve garnished with the fresh basil, if desired.

Nutrition Info:
- Per Serving: Calories: 147;Fat: 6.2g;Protein: 5.2g;Carbs: 20.1g.

Rosemary Garlic Infused Olive Oil

Servings:4
Cooking Time:35 Minutes
Ingredients:
- Salt and black pepper to taste
- 1 cup extra-virgin olive oil
- 4 large garlic cloves, smashed
- 4 sprigs rosemary

Directions:
1. Warm the olive oil in a medium skillet over low heat and sauté garlic and rosemary sprigs for 30-40 minutes, until fragrant and garlic is very tender, stirring occasionally. Don't let the oil get too hot, or the garlic will burn and become bitter. Remove from the heat and leave to cool slightly. Using a slotted spoon, remove the garlic and rosemary and pour the oil into a glass container. Use cooled.

Nutrition Info:
- Per Serving: Calories: 241;Fat: 26.8g;Protein: 0g;Carbs: 1.1g.

Fennel Salad With Olives & Hazelnuts

Servings:4
Cooking Time:5 Minutes
Ingredients:
- 2 tbsp olive oil
- 8 dates, pitted and sliced
- 2 fennel bulbs, sliced
- 2 tbsp chives, chopped
- ½ cup hazelnuts, chopped
- 2 tbsp lime juice
- Salt and black pepper to taste
- 40 green olives, chopped

Directions:
1. Place fennel, dates, chives, hazelnuts, lime juice, olives, olive oil, salt, and pepper in a bowl and toss to combine.

Nutrition Info:
- Per Serving: Calories: 210;Fat: 8g;Protein: 5g;Carbs: 15g.

Italian Vegetable Stew

Servings:4
Cooking Time:25 Minutes
Ingredients:
- 3 zucchini, peeled, chopped
- 1 eggplant, peeled, chopped
- 3 red bell peppers, chopped
- ½ cup fresh tomato juice
- 2 tsp Italian seasoning
- ½ tsp salt
- 2 tbsp olive oil

Directions:

1. Add all ingredients and give it a good stir. Pour 1 cup of water. Seal the lid and cook on High Pressure for 15 minutes. Do a quick release. Set aside to cool completely. Serve as a cold salad or a side dish.

Nutrition Info:
- Per Serving: Calories: 153;Fat: 8.4g;Protein: 4g;Carbs: 20g.

Pork & Mushroom Stew

Servings:2
Cooking Time:50 Minutes
Ingredients:
- 2 pork chops, bones removed and cut into pieces
- 1 cup crimini mushrooms, chopped
- 2 large carrots, chopped
- ½ tsp garlic powder
- Salt and black pepper to taste
- 2 tbsp butter
- 1 cup beef broth
- 1 tbsp apple cider vinegar
- 2 tbsp cornstarch

Directions:
1. Preheat your Instant Pot on Sauté mode. Season the meat with salt and pepper. Add butter and pork chops to the pot and brown for 10 minutes, stirring occasionally. Add mushrooms and cook for 5 minutes. Add the remaining ingredients and seal the lid. Cook on High Pressure for 25 minutes. Do a quick release and serve hot.

Nutrition Info:
- Per Serving: Calories: 451;Fat: 32g;Protein: 22g;Carbs: 17g.

Parsley Carrot & Cabbage Salad

Servings:4
Cooking Time:10 Minutes
Ingredients:
- 2 tbsp olive oil
- 1 green cabbage head, torn
- 1 tbsp lemon juice
- 1 carrot, grated
- Salt and black pepper to taste
- ¼ cup parsley, chopped

Directions:
1. Mix olive oil, lemon juice, carrot, parsley, salt, pepper, and cabbage in a bowl. Serve right away.

Nutrition Info:
- Per Serving: Calories: 110;Fat: 5g;Protein: 5g;Carbs: 5g.

Cucumber & Spelt Salad With Chicken

Servings:4

Cooking Time:35 Minutes

Ingredients:

- 4 tbsp olive oil
- ½ lb chicken breasts
- 1 tbsp dill, chopped
- 2 lemons, zested
- Juice of 2 lemons
- 3 tbsp parsley, chopped
- Salt and black pepper to taste
- 1 cup spelt grains
- 1 red leaf lettuce heads, torn
- 1 red onion, sliced
- 10 cherry tomatoes, halved
- 1 cucumber, sliced

Directions:

1. In a bowl, combine dill, lemon zest, lemon juice, 2 tbsp olive oil, parsley, salt, and pepper and mix well. Add in chicken breasts, toss to coat, cover, and refrigerate for 30 minutes. Place spelt grains in a pot and cover with water. Stir in salt and pepper. Put over medium heat and bring to a boil. Cook for 45 minutes and drain. Transfer to a bowl and let it cool.

2. Preheat the grill. Remove the chicken and grill for 12 minutes on all sides. Transfer to a bowl to cool before slicing. Once the spelt is cooled, add in the remaining olive oil, lettuce, onion, tomatoes, and cucumber and toss to coat. Top the salad with sliced chicken and serve.

Nutrition Info:

- Per Serving: Calories: 350;Fat: 18g;Protein: 27g;Carbs: 28g.

Mixed Salad With Balsamic Honey Dressing

Servings:2

Cooking Time: 0 Minutes

Ingredients:

- Dressing:
- ¼ cup balsamic vinegar
- ¼ cup olive oil
- 1 tablespoon honey
- 1 teaspoon Dijon mustard
- ¼ teaspoon garlic powder
- ¼ teaspoon salt, or more to taste
- Pinch freshly ground black pepper
- Salad:
- 4 cups chopped red leaf lettuce
- ½ cup cherry or grape tomatoes, halved
- ½ English cucumber, sliced in quarters lengthwise and then cut into bite-size pieces
- Any combination fresh, torn herbs (parsley, oregano, basil, or chives)
- 1 tablespoon roasted sunflower seeds

Directions:

1. Make the Dressing
2. Combine the vinegar, olive oil, honey, mustard, garlic powder, salt, and pepper in a jar with a lid. Shake well.
3. Make the Salad
4. In a large bowl, combine the lettuce, tomatoes, cucumber, and herbs. Toss well.
5. Pour all or as much dressing as desired over the tossed salad and toss again to coat the salad with dressing.
6. Top with the sunflower seeds before serving.

Nutrition Info:

- Per Serving: Calories: 337;Fat: 26.1g;Protein: 4.2g;Carbs: 22.2g.

Chicken And Pastina Soup

Servings:6

Cooking Time: 20 Minutes

Ingredients:

- 1 tablespoon extra-virgin olive oil
- 2 garlic cloves, minced
- 3 cups packed chopped kale, center ribs removed
- 1 cup minced carrots
- 8 cups no-salt-added chicken or vegetable broth
- ¼ teaspoon kosher or sea salt
- ¼ teaspoon freshly ground black pepper
- ¾ cup uncooked acini de pepe or pastina pasta
- 2 cups shredded cooked chicken
- 3 tablespoons grated Parmesan cheese

Directions:

1. In a large stockpot over medium heat, heat the oil. Add the garlic and cook for 30 seconds, stirring frequently. Add the kale and carrots and cook for 5 minutes, stirring occasionally.

2. Add the broth, salt, and pepper, and turn the heat to high. Bring the broth to a boil, and add the pasta. Reduce the heat to medium and cook for 10 minutes, or until the pasta is cooked through, stirring every few minutes so the pasta doesn't stick to the bottom. Add the chicken, and cook for another 2 minutes to warm through.

3. Ladle the soup into six bowls. Top each with ½ tablespoon of cheese and serve.

Nutrition Info:

- Per Serving: Calories: 275;Fat: 19.0g;Protein: 16.0g;Carbs: 11.0g.

Easy Spring Salad

Servings:4
Cooking Time:5 Minutes
Ingredients:
- 2 tbsp olive oil
- 2 tomatoes, cut into wedges
- 2 red bell peppers, chopped
- 1 cucumber, chopped
- 1 red onion, sliced
- 8 Kalamata olives, sliced
- ½ cup feta cheese, crumbled
- ¼ cup lime juice
- Salt and black pepper to taste

Directions:
1. Mix tomatoes, bell peppers, cucumber, onion, olives, lime juice, olive oil, salt, and pepper in a bowl. Divide between individual bowls and top with feta cheese to serve.

Nutrition Info:
- Per Serving: Calories: 330;Fat: 12g;Protein: 7g;Carbs: 17g.

Lemony Yogurt Sauce

Servings:4
Cooking Time:5 Minutes
Ingredients:
- 1 cup plain yogurt
- 1 tbsp fresh chives, chopped
- ½ lemon, zested and juiced
- 1 garlic clove, minced
- Salt and black pepper to taste

Directions:
1. Place the yogurt, lemon zest and juice, and garlic in a bowl and mix well. Season with salt and pepper. Let sit for about 30 minutes to blend the flavors. Store in an airtight container in the refrigerator for up to 2-3 days. Serve topped with chives.

Nutrition Info:
- Per Serving: Calories: 258;Fat: 8g;Protein: 8.9g;Carbs: 12.9g.

Mushroom & Bell Pepper Salad

Servings:4
Cooking Time:15 Minutes
Ingredients:
- 2 tbsp olive oil
- ½ lb mushrooms, sliced
- 3 garlic cloves, minced
- Salt and black pepper to taste
- 1 tomato, diced
- 1 red bell pepper, sliced
- 3 tbsp lime juice
- ½ cup chicken stock

- 2 tbsp cilantro, chopped

Directions:
1. Warm the olive oil in a skillet over medium heat and sauté mushrooms for 4 minutes. Stir in garlic, salt, pepper, tomato, bell pepper, lime juice, and chicken stock and sauté for another 4 minutes. Top with cilantro and serve right away.

Nutrition Info:
- Per Serving: Calories: 89;Fat: 7.4g;Protein: 2.5g;Carbs: 5.6g.

Rice Stuffed Bell Peppers

Servings:4
Cooking Time:70 Minutes
Ingredients:
- 4 red bell peppers, tops and seeds removed
- 2 tbsp olive oil
- 1 cup cooked brown rice
- 4 oz crumbled feta cheese
- 4 cups fresh baby spinach
- 3 Roma tomatoes, chopped
- 1 onion, finely chopped
- 1 cup mushrooms, sliced
- 2 garlic cloves, minced
- 1 tsp dried oregano
- Salt and black pepper to taste
- 2 tbsp fresh parsley, chopped

Directions:
1. Preheat oven to 350 F. Warm olive oil in a skillet over medium heat and sauté onion, garlic, and mushrooms for 5 minutes. Stir in tomatoes, spinach, rice, salt, oregano, parsley, and pepper, cook for 3 minutes until the spinach wilts. Remove from the heat. Stuff the bell peppers with the rice mixture and top with feta cheese. Arrange the peppers on a greased baking pan and pour in 1/4 cup of water. Bake covered with aluminum foil for 30 minutes. Then, bake uncovered for another 10 minutes. Serve and enjoy!

Nutrition Info:
- Per Serving: Calories: 387;Fat: 15g;Protein: 12g;Carbs: 55g.

Turkey Egg Soup With Rice

Servings:4
Cooking Time:40 Minutes
Ingredients:
- 2 tbsp olive oil
- 1 lb turkey breasts, cubed
- ½ cup Arborio rice
- 1 onion, chopped
- 1 celery stalk, chopped
- 1 carrot, sliced
- 1 egg
- 2 tbsp yogurt

- 1 tsp dried tarragon
- 1 tsp lemon zest
- 2 tbsp fresh parsley, chopped
- Salt and black pepper to taste

Directions:

1. Heat olive oil in a pot over medium heat and sauté the onion, celery, turkey, and carrot for 6-7 minutes, stirring occasionally. Stir in the rice for 1-2 minutes, pour in 4 cups of water, and season with salt and pepper. Bring the soup to a boil. Lower the heat and simmer for 20 minutes.

2. In a bowl, beat the egg with yogurt until well combined. Remove 1 cup of the hot soup broth with a spoon and add slowly to the egg mixture, stirring constantly. Pour the whisked mixture into the pot and stir in salt, black pepper, tarragon, and lemon zest. Garnish with parsley and serve.

Nutrition Info:

- Per Serving: Calories: 303;Fat: 11g;Protein: 23g;Carbs: 28g.

Home-style Harissa Paste

Servings:4
Cooking Time:10 Minutes
Ingredients:

- 1 tbsp ground dried Aleppo pepper
- 1 tbsp lemon juice
- 2 tbsp tomato paste
- 6 tbsp extra-virgin olive oil
- 6 garlic cloves, minced
- 2 tbsp paprika
- 1 tbsp ground coriander
- 1 tsp ground cumin
- ¾ tsp caraway seeds
- ½ tsp salt

Directions:

1. Microwave the oil, garlic, paprika, coriander, Aleppo pepper, cumin, caraway seeds, and salt for about 1 minute until bubbling and very fragrant, stirring halfway through microwaving. Let cool at room temperature. Store in an airtight container in the refrigerator for up to 2-3 days.

Nutrition Info:

- Per Serving: Calories: 162;Fat: 8.4g;Protein: 4.7g;Carbs: 9g.

Bell Pepper, Tomato & Egg Salad

Servings:4
Cooking Time:15 Min + Chilling Time
Ingredients:

- 4 tbsp olive oil
- 2 hard-boiled eggs, chopped
- 2 cups Greek yogurt
- 1 cup tomatoes, chopped
- 2 mixed bell peppers, sliced
- 1 yellow onion, thinly sliced

- ½ tsp fresh garlic, minced
- 10 Kalamata olives, sliced
- 3 sun-dried tomatoes, chopped
- 1 tbsp fresh lemon juice
- 1 tsp dill, chopped
- 2 tbsp fresh parsley, chopped
- Salt and black pepper to taste

Directions:

1. In a bowl, combine the bell peppers, onion, garlic, Kalamata olives, chopped tomatoes, and sun-dried tomatoes. Stir in the chopped eggs. For the dressing, combine the lemon juice, olive oil, Greek yogurt, dill, salt, and black pepper in a bowl. Pour over the salad and transfer to the fridge to chill. Serve garnished with olives and parsley.

Nutrition Info:

- Per Serving: Calories: 279;Fat: 19g;Protein: 14g;Carbs: 14g.

Tasty Cucumber & Couscous Salad

Servings:4
Cooking Time:30 Minutes
Ingredients:

- ¼ cup olive oil
- 2 tbsp balsamic vinegar
- 1 cup couscous
- 1 cucumber, sliced
- Salt and black pepper to taste
- 2 tbsp lemon juice

Directions:

1. Place couscous in a bowl with 3 cups of hot water and let sit for 10 minutes. Fluff with a fork and remove to a bowl. Stir in cucumber, salt, pepper, lemon juice, vinegar, and olive oil. Serve immediately.

Nutrition Info:

- Per Serving: Calories: 180;Fat: 6g;Protein: 5g;Carbs: 12g.

Salmon & Curly Endive Salad

Servings:4
Cooking Time:5 Minutes
Ingredients:

- 4 oz smoked salmon, flaked
- 2 heads curly endive, torn
- 2 tsp yellow mustard
- ¼ cup lemon juice
- ½ cup Greek yogurt
- Salt and black pepper to taste
- 1 cucumber, sliced
- 2 tbsp chives, chopped

Directions:

1. Toss curly endive, salmon, mustard, lemon juice, yogurt, salt, pepper, cucumber, and chives in a bowl. Serve immediately.

Tomato & Roasted Eggplant Soup

Servings:6
Cooking Time:60 Minutes
Ingredients:
- 2 tbsp olive oil
- 3 eggplants, sliced lengthwise
- Salt to taste
- 1 red onion, chopped
- 2 tbsp garlic, minced
- 1 tsp dried thyme
- Salt and black pepper to taste
- 2 ripe tomatoes, halved
- 5 cups chicken broth
- ¼ cup heavy cream
- 2 tbsp fresh basil, chopped

Directions:
1. Preheat oven to 400 F. Place the eggplants on a greased sheet pan and drizzle with some olive oil. Roast for 45 minutes. Remove from oven and allow to cool. When cool, remove all of the insides, discarding the skins.
2. Warm the remaining olive oil in a large skillet over medium heat. Add the onions and garlic and cook for 5 minutes until soft and translucent. Add the thyme and season with salt and pepper. Put the eggplant, tomatoes, and onion in your food processor and process until smooth. Pour the chicken broth into a pot and bring to a boil. Reduce heat to a simmer and add the eggplant mixture. Stir until well combined and fold in the heavy cream. Adjust to taste. Serve topped with basil.

Nutrition Info:
- Per Serving: Calories: 124;Fat: 5.1g;Protein: 3.5g;Carbs: 19g.

Garlic Herb Butter

Servings:4
Cooking Time:5 Minutes
Ingredients:
- ½ cup butter, softened
- 1 garlic clove, finely minced
- 2 tsp fresh rosemary, chopped
- 1 tsp marjoram, chopped
- Salt to taste

Directions:
1. Blend the butter, garlic, rosemary, marjoram, and salt in your food processor until the mixture is well combined, smooth, and creamy, scraping down the sides as necessary. Scrape the butter mixture with a spatula into a glass container and cover. Store in the refrigerator for up to 30 days.

Green Bean & Rice Chicken Soup

Servings:4
Cooking Time:45 Minutes
Ingredients:
- 2 tbsp olive oil
- 4 cups chicken stock
- ½ lb chicken breasts strips
- 1 celery stalk, chopped
- 2 garlic cloves, minced
- 1 yellow onion, chopped
- ½ cup white rice
- 1 egg, whisked
- ½ lemon, juiced
- 1 cup green beans, chopped
- 1 cup carrots, chopped
- ½ cup dill, chopped
- Salt and black pepper to taste

Directions:
1. Warm the olive oil in a pot over medium heat and sauté onion, garlic, celery, carrots, and chicken for 6-7 minutes.
2. Pour in stock and rice. Bring to a boil and simmer for 10 minutes. Stir in green beans, salt, and pepper and cook for 15 minutes. Whisk the egg and lemon juice and pour into the pot. Stir and cook for 2 minutes. Serve topped with dill.

Nutrition Info:
- Per Serving: Calories: 270;Fat: 19g;Protein: 15g;Carbs: 20g.

Rich Chicken And Small Pasta Broth

Servings:6
Cooking Time: 4 Hours
Ingredients:
- 6 boneless, skinless chicken thighs
- 4 stalks celery, cut into ½-inch pieces
- 4 carrots, cut into 1-inch pieces
- 1 medium yellow onion, halved
- 2 garlic cloves, minced
- 2 bay leaves
- Sea salt and freshly ground black pepper, to taste
- 6 cups low-sodium chicken stock
- ½ cup stelline pasta
- ¼ cup chopped fresh flat-leaf parsley

Directions:
1. Combine the chicken thighs, celery, carrots, onion, and garlic in the slow cooker. Spread with bay leaves and sprinkle with salt and pepper. Toss to mix well.
2. Pour in the chicken stock. Put the lid on and cook on high for 4 hours or until the internal temperature of chicken reaches at least 165°F.

3. In the last 20 minutes of the cooking, remove the chicken from the slow cooker and transfer to a bowl to cool until ready to reserve.

4. Discard the bay leaves and add the pasta to the slow cooker. Put the lid on and cook for 15 minutes or until al dente.

5. Meanwhile, slice the chicken, then put the chicken and parsley in the slow cooker and cook for 5 minutes or until well combined.

6. Pour the soup in a large bowl and serve immediately.

Nutrition Info:
- Per Serving: Calories: 285;Fat: 10.8g;Protein: 27.4g;Carbs: 18.8g.

Arugula & Caper Green Salad

Servings:4
Cooking Time:10 Minutes
Ingredients:
- 1 tbsp olive oil
- 10 green olives, sliced
- 4 cups baby arugula
- 1 tbsp capers, drained
- 1 tbsp balsamic vinegar
- 1 tsp lemon zest, grated
- 1 tbsp lemon juice
- 1 tsp parsley, chopped
- Salt and black pepper to taste

Directions:
1. Mix capers, olives, vinegar, lemon zest, lemon juice, oil, parsley, salt, pepper, and arugula in a bowl. Serve.

Nutrition Info:
- Per Serving: Calories: 160;Fat: 4g;Protein: 5g;Carbs: 4g.

Roasted Pepper & Tomato Soup

Servings:4
Cooking Time:30 Minutes
Ingredients:
- 1 cup roasted bell peppers, chopped
- 2 tbsp olive oil
- 3 tomatoes, cored and halved
- 2 cloves garlic, minced
- 1 yellow onion, quartered
- 1 celery stalk, chopped
- 1 carrot, shredded
- ½ tsp ground cumin
- ½ tsp chili pepper
- 4 cups vegetable broth
- ½ tsp red pepper flakes
- 2 tbsp fresh basil, chopped
- Salt and black pepper to taste
- ¼ cup crème fraîche

Directions:

1. Heat oven to 380 F. Arrange the tomatoes and peppers on a roasting pan. Drizzle olive oil over the vegetables. Roast for 20 minutes until charred. Remove, let cool, and peel them.

2. Heat olive oil in a pot over medium heat and sauté onion, garlic, celery, and carrots for 3-5 minutes until tender. Stir in chili pepper and cumin for 1-2 minutes.

3. Pour in roasted bell peppers and tomatoes, stir, then add in the vegetable broth. Season with salt and pepper. Bring to a boil and reduce the heat; simmer for 10 minutes. Using an immersion blender, purée the soup until smooth. Sprinkle with pepper flakes and basil. Serve topped with crème fraîche.

Nutrition Info:
- Per Serving: Calories: 164;Fat: 12g;Protein: 6.5g;Carbs: 9.8g.

Root Veggie Soup

Servings:4
Cooking Time:40 Minutes
Ingredients:
- 3 cups chopped butternut squash
- 2 tbsp olive oil
- 1 carrot, chopped
- 1 leek, chopped
- 2 garlic cloves, minced
- 1 celery stalk, chopped
- 1 parsnip, chopped
- 1 potato, chopped
- 4 cups vegetable broth
- 1 tsp dried thyme
- Salt and black pepper to taste

Directions:
1. Warm olive oil in a pot over medium heat and sauté leek, garlic, parsnip, carrot, and celery for 5-6 minutes until the veggies start to brown. Throw in squash, potato, broth, thyme, salt, and pepper. Bring to a boil, then decrease the heat and simmer for 20-30 minutes until the veggies soften. Transfer to a food processor and blend until you get a smooth and homogeneous consistency.

Nutrition Info:
- Per Serving: Calories: 200;Fat: 9g;Protein: 7.2g;Carbs: 25.8g.

Marinated Mushrooms And Olives

Servings:8
Cooking Time: 0 Minutes
Ingredients:
- 1 pound white button mushrooms, rinsed and drained
- 1 pound fresh olives
- ½ tablespoon crushed fennel seeds
- 1 tablespoon white wine vinegar
- 2 tablespoons fresh thyme leaves

- Pinch chili flakes
- Sea salt and freshly ground pepper, to taste
- 2 tablespoons extra-virgin olive oil

Directions:

1. Combine all the ingredients in a large bowl. Toss to mix well.
2. Wrap the bowl in plastic and refrigerate for at least 1 hour to marinate.
3. Remove the bowl from the refrigerate and let sit under room temperature for 10 minutes, then serve.

Nutrition Info:

- Per Serving: Calories: 111;Fat: 9.7g;Protein: 2.4g;Carbs: 5.9g.

Portuguese Shrimp Soup

Servings:6
Cooking Time:40 Minutes

Ingredients:

- 1 lb shrimp, shells and tails removed
- 2 tbsp olive oil
- 1 cup green peas
- 1 onion, chopped
- 1 red bell pepper, chopped
- 1 green bell pepper, chopped
- 2 garlic cloves, minced
- 1 tsp ground turmeric
- 1 tsp dried thyme
- 2 tsp smoked paprika
- ½ cup instant brown rice
- 4 cups fish broth
- 1 can diced tomatoes
- 2 tbsp fresh dill, chopped

Directions:

1. Warm the olive oil in a large stockpot over medium heat. Add the onion, red and green bell peppers, and garlic. Cook for 5 minutes, stirring occasionally. Add the turmeric, thyme, and smoked paprika, and cook for another 2 minutes. Stir in the rice and broth. Bring to a boil and simmer for 18-20 minutes. Stir in peas, tomatoes, and shrimp. Cook for 4-6 minutes until the shrimp is cooked. Sprinkle with dill and serve into individual bowls.

Nutrition Info:

- Per Serving: Calories: 275;Fat: 5.2g;Protein: 18g;Carbs: 42g.

Zucchini & Arugula Stuffed Mushrooms

Servings:4
Cooking Time:65 Minutes

Ingredients:

- 4 portobello mushrooms, stems removed
- 2 tbsp olive oil
- 2 cups arugula

- ¼ cup chopped fresh basil
- 1 onion, finely chopped
- 1 zucchini, chopped
- ¼ tsp dried thyme
- ⅛ tsp red pepper flakes
- 2 garlic cloves, minced
- ½ cup grated Parmesan cheese
- Salt and black pepper to taste

Directions:

1. Preheat oven to 350 F. Warm olive oil in a skillet over medium heat and sauté onion, arugula, zucchini, thyme, salt, pepper, and red flakes for 5 minutes. Stir in garlic and sauté for 30 seconds. Turn the heat off. Mix in basil and scoop into the mushroom caps and arrange them on a baking sheet. Top with Parmesan cheese and bake for 30-40 minutes, until mushrooms are nice and soft and cheese is melted.

Nutrition Info:

- Per Serving: Calories: 128;Fat: 8g;Protein: 3g;Carbs: 5.9g.

Zucchini & Green Bean Soup

Servings:4
Cooking Time:30 Minutes

Ingredients:

- 1 ¼ lb green beans, cut into bite-sized chunks
- 2 tbsp olive oil
- 1 onion, chopped
- 1 celery with leaves, chopped
- 1 carrot, chopped
- 2 garlic cloves, minced
- 1 zucchini, chopped
- 5 cups vegetable broth
- 2 tomatoes, chopped
- Salt and black pepper to taste
- ½ tsp cayenne pepper
- 1 tsp oregano
- ½ tsp dried dill
- ½ cup black olives, sliced

Directions:

1. Warm the olive in a pot over medium heat. Sauté the onion, celery, and carrot for about 4 minutes or until the vegetables are just tender. Add in the garlic and zucchini and continue to sauté for 1 minute or until aromatic. Pour in the broth, green beans, tomatoes, salt, black pepper, cayenne pepper, oregano, and dried dill; bring to a boil. Reduce the heat to a simmer and let it cook for about 15 minutes. Serve in individual bowls with sliced olives.

Nutrition Info:

- Per Serving: Calories: 315;Fat: 24g;Protein: 16g;Carbs: 14g.

Chickpea & Broccoli Salad

Servings:6
Cooking Time:10 Minutes
Ingredients:

- ¼ cup extra-virgin olive oil
- 10 oz broccoli florets, steamed
- 2 cans chickpeas
- 15 cherry tomatoes, halved
- ½ red onion, finely chopped
- 2 lemons, juiced and zested
- 2 garlic cloves, minced
- 2 tsp dried oregano
- Salt and black pepper to taste

Directions:

1. Mix the chickpeas, red onion, cherry tomatoes, and broccoli in a bowl. Combine the olive oil, lemon juice, lemon zest, oregano, garlic, salt, and pepper in another bowl. Pour over the salad and toss to combine. Serve immediately.

Nutrition Info:

- Per Serving: Calories: 569;Fat: 16g;Protein: 26g;Carbs: 84g.

Greek-style Pasta Salad

Servings:4
Cooking Time:10 Minutes
Ingredients:

- 2 tbsp olive oil
- 16 oz fusilli pasta
- 1 yellow bell pepper, cubed
- 1 green bell pepper, cubed
- Salt to taste
- 3 tomatoes, cubed
- 1 red onion, sliced
- 2 cups feta cheese, crumbled
- ¼ cup lemon juice
- 1 tbsp lemon zest, grated
- 1 cucumber, cubed
- 1 cup Kalamata olives, sliced

Directions:

1. Cook the fusilli pasta in boiling salted water until "al dente", 8-10 minutes. Drain and set aside to cool. In a bowl, whisk together olive oil, lemon zest, lemon juice, and salt. Add in bell peppers, tomatoes, onion, feta cheese, cucumber, olives, and pasta and toss to combine. Serve.

Nutrition Info:

- Per Serving: Calories: 420;Fat: 18g;Protein: 15g;Carbs: 50g.

Orange Pear Salad With Gorgonzola

Servings:4
Cooking Time:10 Minutes
Ingredients:

- 4 oz gorgonzola cheese, crumbled
- 2 tbsp olive oil
- 1 tsp orange zest
- ¼ cup orange juice
- 3 tbsp balsamic vinegar
- Salt and black pepper to taste
- 1 romaine lettuce head, torn
- 2 pears, cored and cut into medium wedges

Directions:

1. Mix orange zest, orange juice, vinegar, oil, salt, pepper, lettuce, pears, and gorgonzola cheese in a bowl. Serve.

Nutrition Info:

- Per Serving: Calories: 210;Fat: 6g;Protein: 4g;Carbs: 11g.

Turkish Leek & Potato Soup

Servings:5
Cooking Time:30 Minutes
Ingredients:

- 2 tbsp butter
- 1 leek, chopped
- 2 cloves garlic, minced
- 4 cups vegetable broth
- 3 potatoes, peeled and cubed
- ½ cup sour cream
- 2 bay leaves
- Salt and black pepper to taste
- 2 tbsp fresh chives, chopped

Directions:

1. Melt butter on Sauté mode in your Instant Pot. Add in garlic and leeks and cook for 3 to 4 minutes, until soft. Stir in bay leaves, potatoes, and broth. Seal the lid and cook on High Pressure for 15 minutes. Release pressure quickly. Remove the bay leaves and discard. Transfer the soup to a food processor and puree it to obtain a smooth consistency. Season with salt and pepper. Top with chives and sour cream. Serve warm in soup bowls.

Nutrition Info:

- Per Serving: Calories: 287;Fat: 7g;Protein: 6g;Carbs: 51g.

Egg & Potato Salad

Servings:6
Cooking Time:25 Minutes
Ingredients:

- ¼ cup olive oil
- 2 lb potatoes, peeled and sliced
- 4 spring onions, chopped
- ½ cup fennel, sliced
- 2 eggs
- 2 tbsp fresh lemon juice
- 1 tbsp capers
- ½ tbsp Dijon mustard

- Salt and black pepper to taste

Directions:

1. Add the eggs to a pot and cover with salted water. Bring to a boil and turn the heat off. Let sit covered in hot water for 10 minutes, then cool before peeling and cutting into slices. In another pot, place the potatoes and cover them with enough water. Bring to a boil, then lower the heat and simmer for 8-10 minutes until tender.

2. In a serving bowl, whisk the olive oil with lemon juice, mustard, salt, and pepper. Add in the potatoes, eggs, capers, spring onions, and fennel slices and toss to combine. Serve.

Nutrition Info:

- Per Serving: Calories: 183;Fat: 10.6g;Protein: 4g;Carbs: 20g.

Greens, Fennel, And Pear Soup With Cashews

Servings:4

Cooking Time: 15 Minutes

Ingredients:

- 2 tablespoons olive oil
- 1 fennel bulb, cut into ¼-inch-thick slices
- 2 leeks, white part only, sliced
- 2 pears, peeled, cored, and cut into ½-inch cubes
- 1 teaspoon sea salt
- ¼ teaspoon freshly ground black pepper
- ½ cup cashews
- 2 cups packed blanched spinach
- 3 cups low-sodium vegetable soup

Directions:

1. Heat the olive oil in a stockpot over high heat until shimmering.

2. Add the fennel and leeks, then sauté for 5 minutes or until tender.

3. Add the pears and sprinkle with salt and pepper, then sauté for another 3 minutes or until the pears are soft.

4. Add the cashews, spinach, and vegetable soup. Bring to a boil. Reduce the heat to low. Cover and simmer for 5 minutes.

5. Pour the soup in a food processor, then pulse until creamy and smooth.

6. Pour the soup back to the pot and heat over low heat until heated through.

7. Transfer the soup to a large serving bowl and serve immediately.

Nutrition Info:

- Per Serving: Calories: 266;Fat: 15.1g;Protein: 5.2g;Carbs: 32.9g.

Poultry And Meats Recipes

Cannellini Bean & Chicken Cassoulet

Servings:4
Cooking Time:40 Minutes
Ingredients:
- 1 lb chicken thighs, boneless and skinless
- 2 tbsp olive oil
- 2 tbsp tomato paste
- 1 celery stalk, chopped
- 1 sweet onion, chopped
- 2 garlic cloves, chopped
- ½ cup chicken stock
- 14 oz canned cannellini beans
- Salt and black pepper to taste

Directions:
1. Warm the olive oil in a pot over medium heat. Cook onion, celery, and garlic for 3 minutes. Put in chicken and cook for 6 minutes on all sides. Stir in tomato paste, stock, beans, salt, and pepper and bring to a boil. Cook for 30 minutes.

Nutrition Info:
- Per Serving: Calories: 260;Fat: 11g;Protein: 25g;Carbs: 26g.

Vegetable Pork Loin

Servings:4
Cooking Time:30 Minutes
Ingredients:
- 2 tbsp canola oil
- 2 carrots, chopped
- 2 garlic cloves, minced
- 1 lb pork loin, cubed
- 4 oz snow peas
- ¾ cup beef stock
- 1 onion, chopped
- Salt and white pepper to taste

Directions:
1. Warm the oil in a skillet over medium heat and sear pork for 5 minutes. Stir in snow peas, carrots, garlic, stock, onion, salt, and pepper and bring to a boil; cook for 15 minutes.

Nutrition Info:
- Per Serving: Calories: 340;Fat: 18g;Protein: 28g;Carbs: 21g.

Spicy Beef Zoodles

Servings:4
Cooking Time:20 Minutes
Ingredients:

- 2 tbsp olive oil
- 1 lb beef steaks, sliced
- 2 zucchinis, spiralized
- ½ cup sweet chili sauce
- 1 cup carrot, grated
- 3 tbsp water
- Salt and black pepper to taste

Directions:
1. Warm the olive oil in a skillet over medium heat and brown beef steaks for 8 minutes on both side; reserve and cover with foil to keep warm. Stir zucchini noodles, chili sauce, carrot, water, salt, and pepper and cook for an additional 3-4 minutes. Remove the foil from the steaks and pour the zucchini mix over to serve.

Nutrition Info:
- Per Serving: Calories: 360;Fat: 12g;Protein: 37g;Carbs: 26g.

Herb & Pistachio Turkey Breasts

Servings:4
Cooking Time:50 Minutes
Ingredients:
- ½ cup pistachios, toasted and chopped
- 1 tbsp olive oil
- 1 lb turkey breast, cubed
- 1 cup chicken stock
- 1 tbsp basil, chopped
- 1 tbsp rosemary, chopped
- 1 tbsp oregano, chopped
- 1 tbsp parsley, chopped
- 1 tbsp tarragon, chopped
- 3 garlic cloves, minced
- 3 cups tomatoes, chopped

Directions:
1. Warm the olive oil in a skillet over medium heat and cook turkey and garlic for 5 minutes. Stir in stock, basil, rosemary, oregano, parsley, tarragon, pistachios, and tomatoes and bring to a simmer. Cook for 35 minutes. Serve immediately.

Nutrition Info:
- Per Serving: Calories: 310;Fat: 12g;Protein: 25g;Carbs: 20g.

Chicken Bruschetta Burgers

Servings:2
Cooking Time: 16 Minutes
Ingredients:

- 1 tablespoon olive oil
- 2 garlic cloves, minced
- 3 tablespoons finely minced onion
- 1 teaspoon dried basil
- 3 tablespoons minced sun-dried tomatoes packed in olive oil
- 8 ounces ground chicken breast
- ¼ teaspoon salt
- 3 pieces small Mozzarella balls, minced

Directions:

1. Heat the olive oil in a nonstick skillet over medium-high heat. Add the garlic and onion and sauté for 5 minutes until tender. Stir in the basil.
2. Remove from the skillet to a medium bowl.
3. Add the tomatoes, ground chicken, and salt and stir until incorporated. Mix in the Mozzarella balls.
4. Divide the chicken mixture in half and form into two burgers, each about ¾-inch thick.
5. Heat the same skillet over medium-high heat and add the burgers. Cook each side for 5 to 6 minutes, or until they reach an internal temperature of 165ºF.
6. Serve warm.

Nutrition Info:

- Per Serving: Calories: 300;Fat: 17.0g;Protein: 32.2g;Carbs: 6.0g.

Chicken Gyros With Tzatziki Sauce

Servings:2
Cooking Time: 10 Minutes
Ingredients:

- 2 tablespoons freshly squeezed lemon juice
- 2 tablespoons olive oil, divided, plus more for oiling the grill
- 1 teaspoon minced fresh oregano
- ½ teaspoon garlic powder
- Salt, to taste
- 8 ounces chicken tenders
- 1 small eggplant, cut into 1-inch strips lengthwise
- 1 small zucchini, cut into ½-inch strips lengthwise
- ½ red pepper, seeded and cut in half lengthwise
- ½ English cucumber, peeled and minced
- ¾ cup plain Greek yogurt
- 1 tablespoon minced fresh dill
- 2 pita breads

Directions:

1. Combine the lemon juice, 1 tablespoon of olive oil, oregano, garlic powder, and salt in a medium bowl. Add the chicken and let marinate for 30 minutes.

2. Place the eggplant, zucchini, and red pepper in a large mixing bowl and sprinkle with salt and the remaining 1 tablespoon of olive oil. Toss well to coat. Let the vegetables rest while the chicken is marinating.
3. Make the tzatziki sauce: Combine the cucumber, yogurt, salt, and dill in a medium bowl. Stir well to incorporate and set aside in the refrigerator.
4. When ready, preheat the grill to medium-high heat and oil the grill grates.
5. Drain any liquid from the vegetables and put them on the grill.
6. Remove the chicken tenders from the marinade and put them on the grill.
7. Grill the chicken and vegetables for 3 minutes per side, or until the chicken is no longer pink inside.
8. Remove the chicken and vegetables from the grill and set aside. On the grill, heat the pitas for about 30 seconds, flipping them frequently.
9. Divide the chicken tenders and vegetables between the pitas and top each with ¼ cup of the prepared sauce. Roll the pitas up like a cone and serve.

Nutrition Info:

- Per Serving: Calories: 586;Fat: 21.9g;Protein: 39.0g;Carbs: 62.0g.

Apricot-glazed Pork Skewers

Servings:6
Cooking Time:50 Minutes
Ingredients:

- 2 lb pork tenderloin, cubed
- 1 cup apricot jam
- ½ cup apricot nectar
- 1 cup dried whole apricots
- 2 onions, cut into wedges
- ½ tsp dried rosemary

Directions:

1. Coat the pork cubes with apricot jam, cover, and set aside for 10-15 minutes. Bring to a boil the apricot nectar, rosemary, and dried apricots in a saucepan over medium heat. Lower the heat and simmer for 2-3 minutes. Remove the apricots with a perforated spoon and pour the hot liquid over the pork. Stir and drain the pork, reserving the marinade.
2. Preheat your grill to medium-high. Alternate pork cubes, onion wedges, and apricots onto 6 metal skewers. Brush them with some marinade and grill for 10-12 minutes, turning and brushing with some more marinade until the pork is slightly pink and onions are crisp-tender. Simmer the remaining marinade for 3-5 minutes. Serve the skewers with marinade on the side.

Nutrition Info:

- Per Serving: Calories: 393;Fat: 4g;Protein: 34g;Carbs: 59g.

Harissa Beef Burgers

Servings:2
Cooking Time:30 Minutes
Ingredients:
- ½ small onion, minced
- 1 garlic clove, minced
- 1 tsp fresh rosemary, chopped
- Salt and black pepper to taste
- 1 tsp cumin
- 1 tsp smoked paprika
- ¼ tsp ground coriander
- ¼ tsp dried oregano
- 8 oz ground beef
- 2 tbsp olive oil
- 1 cup yogurt
- ½ tsp harissa paste

Directions:
1. Preheat your grill to 350 F. In a bowl, combine the ground beef, onion, garlic, rosemary, salt, pepper, cumin, paprika, oregano, and coriander until is well incorporated. Form the mixture into 2 patties using your hands. Grill the burgers for 6-8 minutes on all sides. Whisk the yogurt and harissa in a small bowl. Serve the burgers with harissa yogurt.

Nutrition Info:
- Per Serving: Calories: 381;Fat: 20g;Protein: 22g;Carbs: 27g.

Easy Pork Stew(2)

Servings:4
Cooking Time:35 Minutes
Ingredients:
- 2 tbsp olive oil
- 1 lb pork shoulder, cubed
- Salt and black pepper to taste
- 1 onion, chopped
- 2 garlic cloves, minced
- 1 tbsp chili paste
- 2 tbsp balsamic vinegar
- ¼ cup chicken stock
- ¼ cup mint, chopped

Directions:
1. Warm the olive oil in a skillet over medium heat and cook onion for 3 minutes. Put in pork cubes and cook for another 3 minutes. Stir in salt, pepper, garlic, chili paste, vinegar, stock, and mint and cook for an additional 20-25 minutes.

Nutrition Info:
- Per Serving: Calories: 310;Fat: 14g;Protein: 20g;Carbs: 16g.

Baked Turkey With Veggies

Servings:4
Cooking Time:70 Minutes
Ingredients:
- 2 tbsp olive oil
- 1 lb turkey breasts, sliced
- ¼ cup chicken stock
- 1 carrot, chopped
- 1 red onion, chopped
- 2 mixed bell peppers, chopped
- Salt and black pepper to taste
- 1 tbsp cilantro, chopped

Directions:
1. Preheat oven to 380 F. Grease a roasting pan with olive oil. Combine turkey, stock, carrots, bell peppers, onion, salt, and pepper in the pan and bake for 1 hour. Top with cilantro.

Nutrition Info:
- Per Serving: Calories: 510;Fat: 15g;Protein: 11g;Carbs: 16g.

Thyme Chicken Roast

Servings:4
Cooking Time:65 Minutes
Ingredients:
- 1 tbsp butter, softened
- 1 lb chicken drumsticks
- 2 garlic cloves, minced
- 1 tsp paprika
- 1 lemon, zested
- 1 tbsp chopped fresh thyme
- Salt and black pepper to taste

Directions:
1. Preheat oven to 350 F. Mix butter, thyme, paprika, salt, garlic, pepper, and lemon zest in a bowl. Rub the mixture all over the chicken drumsticks and arrange them on a baking dish. Add in ½ cup of water and roast in the oven for 50-60 minutes. Remove the chicken from the oven and let it sit covered with foil for 10 minutes. Serve and enjoy!

Nutrition Info:
- Per Serving: Calories: 219;Fat: 9.4g;Protein: 31g;Carbs: 0.5g.

Sautéed Ground Turkey With Brown Rice

Servings:2
Cooking Time: 45 Minutes
Ingredients:
- 1 tablespoon olive oil
- ½ medium onion, minced
- 2 garlic cloves, minced
- 8 ounces ground turkey breast
- ½ cup chopped roasted red peppers,

- ¼ cup sun-dried tomatoes, minced
- 1¼ cups low-sodium chicken stock
- ½ cup brown rice
- 1 teaspoon dried oregano
- Salt, to taste
- 2 cups lightly packed baby spinach

Directions:

1. In a skillet, heat the olive oil over medium heat. Sauté the onion for 5 minutes, stirring occasionally.
2. Stir in the garlic and sauté for 30 seconds more until fragrant.
3. Add the turkey breast and cook for about 7 minutes, breaking apart with a wooden spoon, until the turkey is no longer pink.
4. Stir in the roasted red peppers, tomatoes, chicken stock, brown rice, and oregano and bring to a boil.
5. When the mixture starts to boil, cover, and reduce the heat to medium-low. Bring to a simmer until the rice is tender, stirring occasionally, about 30 minutes. Sprinkle with the salt.
6. Add the baby spinach and keep stirring until wilted.
7. Remove from the heat and serve warm.

Nutrition Info:

- Per Serving: Calories: 445;Fat: 16.8g;Protein: 30.2g;Carbs: 48.9g.

Beef & Bell Pepper Bake

Servings:4
Cooking Time:1 Hour 40 Minutes
Ingredients:

- 2 tbsp olive oil
- 1 lb beef steaks
- 1 red bell pepper, sliced
- 1 green bell pepper, sliced
- 1 yellow bell pepper, sliced
- 2 tbsp oregano, chopped
- 4 garlic cloves, minced
- ½ cup chicken stock
- Salt and black pepper to taste

Directions:

1. Preheat oven to 360 F. Warm olive oil in a skillet over medium heat. Sear the beef steaks for 8 minutes on both sides. Stir in bell peppers, oregano, garlic, stock, salt, and pepper and bake for 80 minutes. Serve warm.

Nutrition Info:

- Per Serving: Calories: 310;Fat: 15g;Protein: 25g;Carbs: 17g.

Pork & Vegetable Gratin

Servings:4
Cooking Time:40 Minutes
Ingredients:

- 3 tbsp olive oil

- 1 lb pork chops
- ½ cup basil leaves, chopped
- ½ cup mint leaves, chopped
- 1 tbsp rosemary, chopped
- 2 garlic cloves, minced
- 1 eggplant, cubed
- 2 zucchinis, cubed
- 1 bell pepper, chopped
- 2 oz mozzarella, crumbled
- 8 oz cherry tomatoes, halved

Directions:

1. Preheat the oven to 380 F. Place pork chops, basil, mint, rosemary, garlic, olive oil, eggplant, zucchinis, bell pepper, and tomatoes in a roasting pan and bake covered with foil for 27 minutes. Uncover, sprinkle with the mozzarella cheese, and bake for another 5-10 minutes until the cheese melts.

Nutrition Info:

- Per Serving: Calories: 340;Fat: 18g;Protein: 25g;Carbs: 19g.

Dragon Pork Chops With Pickle Topping

Servings:4
Cooking Time:30 Minutes
Ingredients:

- ½ cup roasted bell peppers, chopped
- 6 dill pickles, sliced
- 1 cup dill pickle juice
- 6 pork chops, boneless
- Salt and black pepper to taste
- 1 tsp hot pepper sauce
- 1 ½ cups tomatoes, cubed
- 1 jalapeno pepper, chopped
- 10 black olives, sliced

Directions:

1. Place pork chops, hot sauce, and pickle juice in a bowl and marinate in the fridge for 15 minutes. Preheat your grill to High. Remove the chops from the fridge and grill them for 14 minutes on both sides. Combine dill pickles, tomatoes, jalapeño pepper, roasted peppers, and black olives in a bowl. Serve chops topped with the pickle mixture.

Nutrition Info:

- Per Serving: Calories: 230;Fat: 7g;Protein: 36g;Carbs: 7g.

Roasted Pork Tenderloin With Apple Sauce

Servings:4
Cooking Time:35 Minutes
Ingredients:
- 2 tbsp olive oil
- 1 lb pork tenderloin
- Salt and black pepper to taste
- ¼ cup apple jelly
- ¼ cup apple juice
- 2 tbsp wholegrain mustard
- 3 sprigs fresh thyme
- ½ tbsp cornstarch
- ½ tbsp heavy cream

Directions:
1. Preheat oven to 330 F. Warm the oil in a skillet over medium heat. Season the pork with salt and pepper. Sear it for 6-8 minutes on all sides. Transfer to a baking sheet. To the same skillet, add the apple jelly, juice, and mustard and stir for 5 minutes over low heat, stirring often. Top with the pork and thyme sprigs. Place the skillet in the oven and bake for 15-18 minutes, brushing the pork with the apple-mustard sauce every 5 minutes. Remove the pork and let it rest for 15 minutes. Place a small pot over low heat. Blend the cornstarch with heavy cream and cooking juices and pour the mixture into the pot. Stir for 2 minutes until thickens. Drizzle the sauce over the pork. Serve sliced and enjoy!

Nutrition Info:
- Per Serving: Calories: 146;Fat: 7g;Protein: 13g;Carbs: 8g.

Chicken Balls With Yogurt-cucumber Sauce

Servings:4
Cooking Time:40 Minutes
Ingredients:
- 3 tbsp olive oil
- 2 garlic cloves, minced
- 1 lb ground chicken
- 1 egg
- 1 red onion, chopped
- ¼ tsp red pepper flakes
- ½ tsp dried oregano
- 1 cup Greek yogurt
- 1 cucumber, shredded
- ¼ tsp garlic powder
- 2 tbsp lemon juice
- 2 tbsp dill, chopped

Directions:
1. In a bowl, combine ground chicken, egg, red onion, garlic, oregano, and red pepper flakes. Mix to combine well and shape the mixture into 1-inch balls.

2. Preheat the oven to 360 F. Warm 2 tbsp of olive oil in a skillet over medium heat and brown the meatballs for 10 minutes on all sides. Transfer the meatballs to a baking dish and bake for another 15 minutes. Combine Greek yogurt, cucumber, remaining olive oil, garlic powder, lemon juice, and dill in a bowl. Serve the meatballs with yogurt sauce.

Nutrition Info:
- Per Serving: Calories: 380;Fat: 17g;Protein: 24g;Carbs: 27g.

Crispy Pesto Chicken

Servings:2
Cooking Time: 50 Minutes
Ingredients:
- 12 ounces small red potatoes, scrubbed and diced into 1-inch pieces
- 1 tablespoon olive oil
- ½ teaspoon garlic powder
- ¼ teaspoon salt
- 1 boneless, skinless chicken breast
- 3 tablespoons prepared pesto

Directions:
1. Preheat the oven to 425ºF. Line a baking sheet with parchment paper.
2. Combine the potatoes, olive oil, garlic powder, and salt in a medium bowl. Toss well to coat.
3. Arrange the potatoes on the parchment paper and roast for 10 minutes. Flip the potatoes and roast for an additional 10 minutes.
4. Meanwhile, put the chicken in the same bowl and toss with the pesto, coating the chicken evenly.
5. Check the potatoes to make sure they are golden brown on the top and bottom. Toss them again and add the chicken breast to the pan.
6. Turn the heat down to 350ºF and roast the chicken and potatoes for 30 minutes. Check to make sure the chicken reaches an internal temperature of 165ºF and the potatoes are fork-tender.
7. Let cool for 5 minutes before serving.

Nutrition Info:
- Per Serving: Calories: 378;Fat: 16.0g;Protein: 29.8g;Carbs: 30.1g.

Panko Grilled Chicken Patties

Servings:4
Cooking Time: 8 To 10 Minutes
Ingredients:
- 1 pound ground chicken
- 3 tablespoons crumbled feta cheese
- 3 tablespoons finely chopped red pepper
- ¼ cup finely chopped red onion
- 3 tablespoons panko bread crumbs
- 1 garlic clove, minced
- 1 teaspoon chopped fresh oregano

- ¼ teaspoon salt
- ⅛ teaspoon freshly ground black pepper
- Cooking spray

Directions:

1. Mix together the ground chicken, feta cheese, red pepper, red onion, bread crumbs, garlic, oregano, salt, and black pepper in a large bowl, and stir to incorporate.
2. Divide the chicken mixture into 8 equal portions and form each portion into a patty with your hands.
3. Preheat a grill to medium-high heat and oil the grill grates with cooking spray.
4. Arrange the patties on the grill grates and grill each side for 4 to 5 minutes, or until the patties are cooked through.
5. Rest for 5 minutes before serving.

Nutrition Info:

- Per Serving: Calories: 241;Fat: 13.5g;Protein: 23.2g;Carbs: 6.7g.

Greek-style Chicken & Egg Bake

Servings:4
Cooking Time:45 Minutes

Ingredients:

- ½ lb Halloumi cheese, grated
- 1 tbsp olive oil
- 1 lb chicken breasts, cubed
- 4 eggs, beaten
- 1 tsp dry mustard
- 2 cloves garlic, crushed
- 2 red bell peppers, sliced
- 1 red onion, sliced
- 2 tomatoes, chopped
- 1 tsp sweet paprika
- ½ tsp dried basil
- Salt to taste

Directions:

1. Preheat oven to 360 F. Warm the olive oil in a skillet over medium heat. Add the bell peppers, garlic, onion, and salt and cook for 3 minutes. Stir in tomatoes for an additional 5 minutes. Put in chicken breasts, paprika, dry mustard, and basil. Cook for another 6-8 minutes. Transfer the mixture to a greased baking pan and pour over the beaten eggs; season with salt. Bake for 15-18 minutes. Remove and spread the cheese over the top. Let cool for a few minutes. Serve sliced.

Nutrition Info:

- Per Serving: Calories: 480;Fat: 31g;Protein: 39g;Carbs: 12g.

Chicken Thighs With Roasted Artichokes

Servings:4
Cooking Time:25 Minutes
Ingredients:

- 2 artichoke hearts, halved lengthwise
- 2 tbsp butter, melted
- 3 tbsp olive oil
- 2 lemons, zested and juiced
- ½ tsp salt
- 4 chicken thighs

Directions:

1. Preheat oven to 450 F. Place a large, rimmed baking sheet in the oven. Whisk the olive oil, lemon zest, and lemon juice in a bowl. Add the artichoke hearts and turn them to coat on all sides. Lay the artichoke halves flat-side down in the center of 4 aluminum foil sheets and close up loosely to create packets. Put the chicken in the remaining lemon mixture and toss to coat. Carefully remove the hot baking sheet from the oven and pour on the butter; tilt the pan to coat.
2. Arrange the chicken thighs, skin-side down, on the sheet, add the artichoke packets. Roast for about 20 minutes or until the chicken is cooked through and the skin is slightly charred. Check the artichokes for doneness and bake for another 5 minutes if needed. Serve and enjoy!

Nutrition Info:

- Per Serving: Calories: 832;Fat: 80g;Protein: 19g;Carbs: 11g.

Parsley-dijon Chicken And Potatoes

Servings:6
Cooking Time: 22 Minutes
Ingredients:

- 1 tablespoon extra-virgin olive oil
- 1½ pounds boneless, skinless chicken thighs, cut into 1-inch cubes, patted dry
- 1½ pounds Yukon Gold potatoes, unpeeled, cut into ½-inch cubes
- 2 garlic cloves, minced
- ¼ cup dry white wine
- 1 cup low-sodium or no-salt-added chicken broth
- 1 tablespoon Dijon mustard
- ¼ teaspoon freshly ground black pepper
- ¼ teaspoon kosher or sea salt
- 1 cup chopped fresh flat-leaf (Italian) parsley, including stems
- 1 tablespoon freshly squeezed lemon juice

Directions:

1. In a large skillet over medium-high heat, heat the oil. Add the chicken and cook for 5 minutes, stirring only after the chicken has browned on one side. Remove the chicken and reserve on a plate.
2. Add the potatoes to the skillet and cook for 5 minutes, stirring only after the potatoes have become golden and crispy on one side. Push the potatoes to the side of the skillet, add the garlic, and cook, stirring constantly, for 1 minute. Add the wine and cook for 1 minute, until nearly evaporated.

Add the chicken broth, mustard, salt, pepper, and reserved chicken. Turn the heat to high and bring to a boil.

3. Once boiling, cover, reduce the heat to medium-low, and cook for 10 to 12 minutes, until the potatoes are tender and the internal temperature of the chicken measures 165ºF on a meat thermometer and any juices run clear.

4. During the last minute of cooking, stir in the parsley. Remove from the heat, stir in the lemon juice, and serve.

Nutrition Info:
- Per Serving: Calories: 324;Fat: 9.0g;Protein: 16.0g;Carbs: 45.0g.

Rosemary Fennel In Cherry Tomato Sauce

Servings:4
Cooking Time:20 Minutes
Ingredients:
- 2 tbsp olive oil
- ½ tsp garlic, minced
- Salt and black pepper to taste
- ¼ cup vegetable broth
- 1 fennel, thinly sliced
- For the Sauce:
- 1 cup cherry tomatoes
- 2 tbsp fresh basil, chopped
- 1 tsp rosemary
- ½ cup red onion, chopped
- 1 tsp oregano
- 2 tbsp olive oil
- 1 cloves garlic, minced
- 1 cayenne pepper, minced
- Salt and black pepper to taste

Directions:
1. Warm the olive oil in a pan over medium heat. Sauté the garlic until aromatic. Add in the fennel, broth, salt, and pepper and cook until the fennel is just tender; remove to a plate. Puree the sauce ingredients in your food processor until smooth and creamy. Pour the sauce into a pan over medium heat and cook for 5-6 minutes. Pour the sauce over the fennel and serve.

Nutrition Info:
- Per Serving: Calories: 138;Fat: 14g;Protein: 1g;Carbs: 3g.

Thyme Zucchini & Chicken Stir-fry

Servings:4
Cooking Time:40 Minutes
Ingredients:
- 2 tbsp olive oil
- 2 cups tomatoes, crushed
- 1 lb chicken breasts, cubed
- Salt and black pepper to taste
- 2 shallots, sliced

- 3 garlic cloves, minced
- 2 zucchinis, sliced
- 2 tbsp thyme, chopped
- 1 cup chicken stock

Directions:
1. Warm the olive oil in a skillet over medium heat. Sear chicken for 6 minutes, stirring occasionally. Add in shallots and garlic and cook for another 4 minutes. Stir in tomatoes, salt, pepper, zucchinis, and stock and bring to a boil; simmer for 20 minutes. Garnish with thyme and serve.

Nutrition Info:
- Per Serving: Calories: 240;Fat: 10g;Protein: 19;Carbs: 17g.

Easy Grilled Pork Chops

Servings:4
Cooking Time: 10 Minutes
Ingredients:
- ¼ cup extra-virgin olive oil
- 2 tablespoons fresh thyme leaves
- 1 teaspoon smoked paprika
- 1 teaspoon salt
- 4 pork loin chops, ½-inch-thick

Directions:
1. In a small bowl, mix together the olive oil, thyme, paprika, and salt.

2. Put the pork chops in a plastic zip-top bag or a bowl and coat them with the spice mix. Let them marinate for 15 minutes.

3. Preheat the grill to high heat. Cook the pork chops for 4 minutes on each side until cooked through.

4. Serve warm.

Nutrition Info:
- Per Serving: Calories: 282;Fat: 23.0g;Protein: 21.0g;Carbs: 1.0g.

Ground Beef, Tomato, And Kidney Bean Chili

Servings:4
Cooking Time: 15 Minutes
Ingredients:
- 1 tablespoon extra-virgin olive oil
- 1 pound extra-lean ground beef
- 1 onion, chopped
- 2 cans kidney beans
- 2 cans chopped tomatoes, juice reserved
- Simple Chili Spice:
- 1 teaspoon garlic powder
- 1 tablespoon chili powder
- ½ teaspoon sea salt

Directions:
1. Heat the olive oil in a pot over medium-high heat until shimmering.

2. Add the beef and onion to the pot and sauté for 5 minutes or until the beef is lightly browned and the onion is translucent.

3. Add the remaining ingredients. Bring to a boil. Reduce the heat to medium and cook for 10 more minutes. Keep stirring during the cooking.

4. Pour them in a large serving bowl and serve immediately.

Nutrition Info:

• Per Serving: Calories: 891;Fat: 20.1g;Protein: 116.3g;Carbs: 62.9g.

Lamb Tagine With Couscous And Almonds

Servings:6
Cooking Time: 7 Hours 7 Minutes
Ingredients:

• 2 tablespoons almond flour
• Juice and zest of 1 navel orange
• 2 tablespoons extra-virgin olive oil
• 2 pounds boneless lamb leg, fat trimmed and cut into 1½-inch cubes
• ½ cup low-sodium chicken stock
• 2 large white onions, chopped
• 1 teaspoon pumpkin pie spice
• ¼ teaspoon crushed saffron threads
• 1 teaspoon ground cumin
• ¼ teaspoon ground red pepper flakes
• ½ teaspoon sea salt
• 2 tablespoons raw honey
• 1 cup pitted dates
• 3 cups cooked couscous, for serving
• 2 tablespoons toasted slivered almonds, for serving

Directions:

1. Combine the almond flour with orange juice in a large bowl. Stir until smooth, then mix in the orange zest. Set aside.

2. Heat the olive oil in a nonstick skillet over medium-high heat until shimmering.

3. Add the lamb cubes and sauté for 7 minutes or until lightly browned.

4. Pour in the flour mixture and chicken stock, then add the onions, pumpkin pie spice, saffron, cumin, ground red pepper flakes, and salt. Stir to mix well.

5. Pour them in the slow cooker. Cover and cook on low for 6 hours or until the internal temperature of the lamb reaches at least 145ºF.

6. When the cooking is complete, mix in the honey and dates, then cook for another an hour.

7. Put the couscous in a tagine bowl or a simple large bowl, then top with lamb mixture. Scatter with slivered almonds and serve immediately.

Nutrition Info:

• Per Serving: Calories: 447;Fat: 10.2g;Protein: 36.3g;Carbs: 53.5g.

Catalan Chicken In Romesco Sauce

Servings:6
Cooking Time:25 Minutes
Ingredients:

• 1 ½ lb chicken breasts, sliced
• 1 carrot, halved
• 1 celery stalk, halved
• 2 shallots, halved
• 2 garlic cloves, smashed
• 3 sprigs fresh thyme
• 1 cup romesco sauce
• 2 tbsp parsley, chopped
• ¼ tsp black pepper

Directions:

1. Place the chicken in a saucepan, cover well with water, and add the carrot, celery, onion, garlic, and thyme. Bring to the boil, then turn down to low and poach for 10-15 minutes until cooked through with no pink showing. Remove the chicken from the saucepan and leave to cool for 5 minutes. Spread some romesco sauce on the bottom of a serving plate. Arrange the chicken slices on top, and drizzle with the remaining romesco sauce. Sprinkle the tops with parsley and black pepper. Serve and enjoy!

Nutrition Info:

• Per Serving: Calories: 270;Fat: 11g;Protein: 13g;Carbs: 31g.

Portuguese-style Chicken Breasts

Servings:4
Cooking Time:45 Minutes
Ingredients:

• 2 tbsp avocado oil
• 1 lb chicken breasts, cubed
• Salt and black pepper to taste
• 1 red onion, chopped
• 15 oz canned chickpeas
• 15 oz canned tomatoes, diced
• 1 cup Kalamata olives, pitted and halved
• 2 tbsp lime juice
• 1 tsp cilantro, chopped

Directions:

1. Warm the olive oil in a pot over medium heat and sauté chicken and onion for 5 minutes. Put in salt, pepper, chickpeas, tomatoes, olives, lime juice, cilantro, and 2 cups of water. Cover with lid and bring to a boil, then reduce the heat and simmer for 30 minutes. Serve warm.

Nutrition Info:

• Per Serving: Calories: 360;Fat: 16g;Protein: 28g;Carbs: 26g.

Spicy Mustard Pork Tenderloin

Servings:4
Cooking Time:30 Minutes
Ingredients:
- 2 tbsp olive oil
- 1 pork tenderloin
- 2 garlic cloves, minced
- ½ cup fresh parsley, chopped
- 1 tbsp rosemary, chopped
- 1 tbsp tarragon, chopped
- 3 tbsp stone-ground mustard
- ½ tsp cumin powder
- ½ chili pepper, minced
- Salt and black pepper to taste

Directions:
1. Preheat oven to 400 F. In a food processor, blend parsley, tarragon, rosemary, mustard, olive oil, chili pepper, cumin, salt, garlic, and pepper until smooth. Rub the mixture all over the pork and transfer onto a lined baking sheet. Bake in the oven for 20-25 minutes. Slice and serve.

Nutrition Info:
- Per Serving: Calories: 970;Fat: 29g;Protein: 16g;Carbs: 2.6g.

Picante Beef Stew

Servings:4
Cooking Time:35 Minutes
Ingredients:
- 2 tbsp olive oil
- 1 carrot, chopped
- 4 potatoes, diced
- 1 tsp ground nutmeg
- ½ tsp cinnamon
- 1 lb beef stew meat, cubed
- ½ cup sweet chili sauce
- ½ cup vegetable stock
- 1 tbsp cilantro, chopped
- Salt and black pepper to taste

Directions:
1. Warm the olive oil in a skillet over medium heat and sear beef for 5 minutes. Stir in chili sauce, carrot, potatoes, stock, nutmeg, cinnamon, cilantro, salt, and pepper and bring to a boil. Cook for another 20 minutes. Serve immediately.

Nutrition Info:
- Per Serving: Calories: 300;Fat: 22g;Protein: 20g;Carbs: 26g.

Coriander Pork Roast

Servings:4
Cooking Time:2 Hours 10 Minutes
Ingredients:
- 2 tbsp olive oil
- 2 lb pork loin roast, boneless
- Salt and black pepper to taste
- 2 garlic cloves, minced
- 1 tsp ground coriander
- 1 tbsp coriander seeds
- 2 tsp red pepper, crushed

Directions:
1. Preheat the oven to 360 F. Toss pork, salt, pepper, garlic, ground coriander, coriander seeds, red pepper, and olive oil in a roasting pan and bake for 2 hours. Serve sliced.

Nutrition Info:
- Per Serving: Calories: 310;Fat: 5g;Protein: 16g;Carbs: 7g.

Saucy Turkey With Ricotta Cheese

Servings:4
Cooking Time:60 Minutes
Ingredients:
- 2 tbsp olive oil
- 1 turkey breast, cubed
- 1 ½ cups salsa verde
- Salt and black pepper to taste
- 4 oz ricotta cheese, crumbled
- 2 tbsp cilantro, chopped

Directions:
1. Preheat the oven to 380 F. Grease a roasting pan with oil. In a bowl, place turkey, salsa verde, salt, and pepper and toss to coat. Transfer to the roasting pan and bake for 50 minutes. Top with ricotta cheese and cilantro and serve.

Nutrition Info:
- Per Serving: Calories: 340;Fat: 16g;Protein: 35g;Carbs: 23g.

Peppery Chicken Bake

Servings:4
Cooking Time:70 Minutes
Ingredients:
- 3 tbsp olive oil
- 1 lb chicken breasts, sliced
- 2 lb cherry tomatoes, halved
- 1 onion, chopped
- 3 garlic cloves, minced
- 3 red chili peppers, chopped
- ½ lemon, zested
- Salt and black pepper to taste

Directions:
1. Warm the olive oil in a skillet over medium heat and brown chicken for 8 minutes on both sides. Remove to a roasting pan. In the same skillet, add onion, garlic, and chili peppers and cook for 2 minutes. Pour the mixture over the chicken and toss to coat. Add in tomatoes, lemon zest, 1 cup

of water, salt, and pepper. Bake for 45 minutes. Serve and enjoy!

Nutrition Info:

- Per Serving: Calories: 280;Fat: 14g;Protein: 34g;Carbs: 25g.

Fennel Beef Ribs

Servings:4
Cooking Time:2 Hours 10 Minutes
Ingredients:

- 2 tbsp olive oil
- 2 lb beef ribs
- 2 garlic cloves, minced
- 1 onion, chopped
- ½ cup chicken stock
- 1 tbsp ground fennel seeds

Directions:

1. Preheat oven to 360 F. Mix garlic, onion, stock, olive oil, fennel seeds, and beef ribs in a roasting pan and bake for 2 hours. Serve hot with salad.

Nutrition Info:

- Per Serving: Calories: 300;Fat: 10g;Protein: 25g;Carbs: 18g.

Milky Pork Stew

Servings:4
Cooking Time:50 Minutes
Ingredients:

- 1 tbsp avocado oil
- 1 ½ cups buttermilk
- 1 ½ lb pork meat, cubed
- 1 red onion, chopped
- 1 garlic clove, minced
- ½ cup chicken stock
- 2 tbsp hot paprika
- Salt and black pepper to taste
- 1 tbsp cilantro, chopped

Directions:

1. Warm the avocado oil in a pot over medium heat and sear pork for 5 minutes. Put in onion and garlic and cook for 5 minutes. Stir in stock, paprika, salt, pepper, and buttermilk and bring to a boil; cook for 30 minutes. Top with cilantro.

Nutrition Info:

- Per Serving: Calories: 310;Fat: 10g;Protein: 23g;Carbs: 16g.

Grilled Beef With Mint-jalapeño Vinaigrette

Servings:4
Cooking Time:25 Minutes
Ingredients:

- 2 tbsp olive oil
- 1 lb beef steaks

- 3 jalapeños, chopped
- 2 tbsp balsamic vinegar
- 1 cup mint leaves, chopped
- Salt and black pepper to taste
- 1 tbsp sweet paprika

Directions:

1. Warm half of oil in a skillet over medium heat and sauté jalapeños, balsamic vinegar, mint, salt, pepper, and paprika for 5 minutes. Preheat the grill to high. Rub beef steaks with the remaining oil, salt, and pepper and grill for 6 minutes on both sides. Top with mint vinaigrette and serve.

Nutrition Info:

- Per Serving: Calories: 320;Fat: 13g;Protein: 18g;Carbs: 19g.

Beef & Vegetable Stew

Servings:6
Cooking Time:and Total Time: 35 Minutes
Ingredients:

- 2 sweet potatoes, cut into chunks
- 2 lb beef meat for stew
- ¾ cup red wine
- 1 tbsp butter
- 6 oz tomato paste
- 6 oz baby carrots, chopped
- 1 onion, finely chopped
- Salt to taste
- 4 cups beef broth
- ½ cup green peas
- 1 tsp dried thyme
- 3 garlic cloves, crushed

Directions:

1. Heat the butter on Sauté in your Instant pot. Add beef and brown for 5-6 minutes. Add onions and garlic, and keep stirring for 3 more minutes. Add the remaining ingredients and seal the lid. Cook on Meat/Stew for 20 minutes on High pressure. Do a quick release and serve immediately.

Nutrition Info:

- Per Serving: Calories: 470;Fat: 15g;Protein: 51g;Carbs: 27g.

Almond-crusted Chicken Tenders With Honey

Servings:4
Cooking Time: 20 Minutes
Ingredients:

- 1 tablespoon honey
- 1 tablespoon whole-grain or Dijon mustard
- ¼ teaspoon freshly ground black pepper
- ¼ teaspoon kosher or sea salt
- 1 pound boneless, skinless chicken breast tenders or tenderloins

- 1 cup almonds, roughly chopped
- Nonstick cooking spray

Directions:

1. Preheat the oven to 425ºF. Line a large, rimmed baking sheet with parchment paper. Place a wire cooling rack on the parchment-lined baking sheet, and spray the rack well with nonstick cooking spray.

2. In a large bowl, combine the honey, mustard, pepper, and salt. Add the chicken and toss gently to coat. Set aside.

3. Dump the almonds onto a large sheet of parchment paper and spread them out. Press the coated chicken tenders into the nuts until evenly coated on all sides. Place the chicken on the prepared wire rack.

4. Bake in the preheated oven for 15 to 20 minutes, or until the internal temperature of the chicken measures 165ºF on a meat thermometer and any juices run clear.

5. Cool for 5 minutes before serving.

Nutrition Info:

- Per Serving: Calories: 222;Fat: 7.0g;Protein: 11.0g;Carbs: 29.0g.

Pork Chops In Wine Sauce

Servings:4
Cooking Time:30 Minutes

Ingredients:

- 2 tbsp olive oil
- 4 pork chops
- 1 cup red onion, sliced
- 10 black peppercorns, crushed
- ¼ cup vegetable stock
- ¼ cup dry white wine
- 2 garlic cloves, minced
- Salt to taste

Directions:

1. Warm the olive oil in a skillet over medium heat and sear pork chops for 8 minutes on both sides. Put in onion and garlic and cook for another 2 minutes. Mix in stock, wine, salt, and peppercorns and cook for 10 minutes, stirring often.

Nutrition Info:

- Per Serving: Calories: 240;Fat: 10g;Protein: 25g;Carbs: 14g.

Fruits, Desserts And Snacks Recipes

Avocado & Salmon Stuffed Cucumbers

Servings:4
Cooking Time:10 Minutes
Ingredients:

- 1 tbsp extra-virgin olive oil
- 2 large cucumbers, peeled
- 1 can red salmon
- 1 ripe avocado, mashed
- 2 tbsp chopped fresh dill
- Salt and black pepper to taste

Directions:

1. Cut the cucumber into 1-inch-thick segments, and using a spoon, scrape seeds out of the center of each piece and stand up on a plate. In a bowl, mix the salmon, avocado, olive oil, lime zest and juice, dill, salt, and pepper, and blend until creamy. Spoon the salmon mixture into the center of each cucumber segment and serve chilled.

Nutrition Info:

- Per Serving: Calories: 159;Fat: 11g;Protein: 9g;Carbs: 8g.

Poached Pears In Red Wine

Servings:4
Cooking Time:1 Hour 35 Minutes
Ingredients:

- 4 pears, peeled with stalk intact
- 2 cups red wine
- 8 whole cloves
- 1 cinnamon stick
- ½ tsp vanilla extract
- 2 tsp sugar
- Creme fraiche for garnish

Directions:

1. In a pot over low heat, mix red wine, cinnamon stick, cloves, vanilla, and sugar and bring to a simmer, stirring often until the sugar is dissolved. Add in the pears, make sure that they are submerged and poach them for 15-20 minutes.
2. Remove the pears to a platter and allow the liquid simmering over medium heat for 15 minutes until reduced by half and syrupy. Remove from the heat and let cool for 10 minutes. Drain to discard the spices, let cool, and pour over the pears. Top with creme fraiche and serve.

Nutrition Info:

- Per Serving: Calories: 158;Fat: 1g;Protein: 2g;Carbs: 33g.

The Best Trail Mix

Servings:4
Cooking Time:20 Minutes
Ingredients:

- 1 tbsp olive oil
- 1 tbsp maple syrup
- 1 tsp vanilla
- ½ tsp paprika
- ½ tsp cardamom
- ½ tsp allspice
- 2 cups mixed, unsalted nuts
- ¼ cup sunflower seeds
- ½ cup dried apricots, diced
- ½ cup dried figs, diced
- Salt to taste

Directions:

1. Mix the olive oil, maple syrup, vanilla, cardamom, paprika, and allspice in a pan over medium heat. Stir to combine. Add the nuts and seeds and stir well to coat. Let the nuts and seeds toast for about 10 minutes, stirring often. Remove from the heat, and add the dried apricots and figs. Stir everything well and season with salt. Store in an airtight container.

Nutrition Info:

- Per Serving: Calories: 261;Fat: 18g;Protein: 6g;Carbs: 23g.

Strawberry Parfait

Servings:2
Cooking Time:10 Minutes
Ingredients:

- ¾ cup Greek yogurt
- 1 tbsp cocoa powder
- ¼ cup strawberries, chopped
- 5 drops vanilla stevia

Directions:

1. Combine cocoa powder, strawberries, yogurt, and stevia in a bowl. Serve immediately.

Nutrition Info:

- Per Serving: Calories: 210;Fat: 9g;Protein: 5g;Carbs: 8g.

Greek Yogurt Affogato With Pistachios

Servings:4
Cooking Time: 0 Minutes
Ingredients:
- 24 ounces vanilla Greek yogurt
- 2 teaspoons sugar
- 4 shots hot espresso
- 4 tablespoons chopped unsalted pistachios
- 4 tablespoons dark chocolate chips

Directions:
1. Spoon the yogurt into four bowls or tall glasses.
2. Mix ½ teaspoon of sugar into each of the espresso shots.
3. Pour one shot of the hot espresso over each bowl of yogurt.
4. Top each bowl with 1 tablespoon of the pistachios and 1 tablespoon of the chocolate chips and serve.

Nutrition Info:
- Per Serving: Calories: 190;Fat: 6.0g;Protein: 20.0g;Carbs: 14.0g.

Balsamic Squash Wedges With Walnuts

Servings:4
Cooking Time:50 Minutes
Ingredients:
- 3 tbsp olive oil
- 1 lb butternut squash, peeled and cut into wedges
- 1 cup walnuts, chopped
- 1 tbsp chili paste
- 1 tbsp balsamic vinegar
- 1 tbsp chives, chopped

Directions:
1. Preheat the oven to 380 F. Line a baking sheet with parchment paper. Combine squash wedges, chili paste, olive oil, vinegar, and chives in a bowl and arrange on the sheet. Bake for 40 minutes, turning often. Sprinkle with walnuts.

Nutrition Info:
- Per Serving: Calories: 190;Fat: 5g;Protein: 2g;Carbs: 7g.

Turkish Baklava

Servings:6
Cooking Time:40 Min + Chilling Time
Ingredients:
- 20 sheets phyllo pastry dough, at room temperature
- 1 cup butter, melted
- 1 ½ cups chopped walnuts
- 1 tsp ground cinnamon
- ¼ tsp ground cardamom
- ½ cup sugar
- ½ cup honey
- 2 tbsp lemon juice
- 1 tbsp lemon zest

Directions:
1. In a small pot, bring 1 cup of water, sugar, honey, lemon zest, and lemon juice just to a boil. Remove and let cool.
2. Preheat oven to 350 F. In a small bowl, mix the walnuts, cinnamon, and cardamom and set aside. Put the butter in a small bowl. Put 1 layer of phyllo dough on a baking sheet and slowly brush with butter. Carefully layer 2 more phyllo sheets, brushing each with butter in the baking pan and then layer 1 tbsp of the nut mix; layer 2 sheets and add another 1 tbsp of the nut mix; repeat with 2 sheets and nuts until you run out of nuts and dough, topping with the remaining phyllo dough sheets. Slice 4 lines into the baklava lengthwise and make another 4 or 5 slices diagonally across the pan. Bake for 30-40 minutes or until golden brown. Remove the baklava from the oven and immediately cover it with the syrup. Let cool and serve.

Nutrition Info:
- Per Serving: Calories: 443;Fat: 27g;Protein: 6g;Carbs: 47g.

Simple Peanut Butter And Chocolate Balls

Servings:15
Cooking Time: 0 Minutes
Ingredients:
- ¾ cup creamy peanut butter
- ¼ cup unsweetened cocoa powder
- 2 tablespoons softened almond butter
- ½ teaspoon vanilla extract
- 1¾ cups maple sugar

Directions:
1. Line a baking sheet with parchment paper.
2. Combine all the ingredients in a bowl. Stir to mix well.
3. Divide the mixture into 15 parts and shape each part into a 1-inch ball.
4. Arrange the balls on the baking sheet and refrigerate for at least 30 minutes, then serve chilled.

Nutrition Info:
- Per Serving: Calories: 146;Fat: 8.1g;Protein: 4.2g;Carbs: 16.9g.

Easy Blueberry And Oat Crisp

Servings:4
Cooking Time: 20 Minutes
Ingredients:
- 2 tablespoons coconut oil, melted, plus additional for greasing
- 4 cups fresh blueberries
- Juice of ½ lemon
- 2 teaspoons lemon zest
- ¼ cup maple syrup

- 1 cup gluten-free rolled oats
- ½ cup chopped pecans
- ½ teaspoon ground cinnamon
- Sea salt, to taste

Directions:

1. Preheat the oven to 350ºF. Grease a baking sheet with coconut oil.
2. Combine the blueberries, lemon juice and zest, and maple syrup in a bowl. Stir to mix well, then spread the mixture on the baking sheet.
3. Combine the remaining ingredients in a small bowl. Stir to mix well. Pour the mixture over the blueberries mixture.
4. Bake in the preheated oven for 20 minutes or until the oats are golden brown.
5. Serve immediately with spoons.

Nutrition Info:

- Per Serving: Calories: 496;Fat: 32.9g;Protein: 5.1g;Carbs: 50.8g.

Roasted Eggplant Hummus

Servings:4
Cooking Time:25 Minutes

Ingredients:

- 1 lb eggplants, peeled and sliced
- 1 lemon, juiced
- 1 garlic clove, minced
- ¼ cup tahini
- ¼ tsp ground cumin
- Salt and black pepper to taste
- 2 tbsp fresh parsley, chopped
- ½ cup mayonnaise

Directions:

1. Preheat oven to 350 F. Arrange the eggplant slices on a baking sheet and bake for 15 minutes until tender. Let cool slightly before chopping. In a food processor, mix eggplants, salt, lemon juice, tahini, cumin, garlic, and pepper for 30 seconds. Remove to a bowl. Stir in mayonnaise. Serve topped with parsley.

Nutrition Info:

- Per Serving: Calories: 235;Fat: 18g;Protein: 4.1g;Carbs: 17g.

Turkish Dolma (stuffed Grape Leaves)

Servings:4
Cooking Time:50 Minutes

Ingredients:

- 2 tbsp olive oil
- 1 onion, chopped
- 2 garlic cloves, minced
- 1 cup short-grain rice
- ¼ cup gold raisins
- ¼ cup pine nuts, toasted

- 1 lemon, juiced
- ¼ tsp ground cinnamon
- Salt and black pepper to taste
- 2 tbsp parsley, chopped
- 20 preserved grape leaves

Directions:

1. Warm the olive oil in a skillet over medium heat. Add the onion and garlic and sauté for 5 minutes. Add the rice, golden raisins, pine nuts, cinnamon, and lemon juice. Season with salt and pepper. Stuff each leaf with about 1 tablespoon of the filling. Roll tightly and place each in a pot, seam side down. Add 2 cups of water and simmer for about 15-18 minutes. Serve warm.

Nutrition Info:

- Per Serving: Calories: 237;Fat: 12g;Protein: 7g;Carbs: 26g.

Chili Grilled Eggplant Rounds

Servings:4
Cooking Time:25 Minutes

Ingredients:

- 1 cup roasted peppers, chopped
- 4 tbsp olive oil
- 2 eggplants, cut into rounds
- 12 Kalamata olives, chopped
- 1 tsp red chili flakes, crushed
- Salt and black pepper to taste
- 2 tbsp basil, chopped
- 2 tbsp Parmesan cheese, grated

Directions:

1. Combine roasted peppers, half of the olive oil, olives, red chili flakes, salt, and pepper in a bowl. Rub each eggplant slice with remaining olive oil and salt grill them on the preheated grill for 14 minutes on both sides. Remove to a platter. Distribute the pepper mixture across the eggplant rounds and top with basil and Parmesan cheese to serve.

Nutrition Info:

- Per Serving: Calories: 220;Fat: 11g;Protein: 6g;Carbs: 16g.

Vegetarian Spinach-olive Pizza

Servings:4
Cooking Time:40 Minutes

Ingredients:

- For the crust
- 1 tbsp olive oil
- ½ cup almond flour
- ¼ tsp salt
- 2 tbsp ground psyllium husk
- 1 cup lukewarm water
- For the topping
- ½ cup tomato sauce
- ½ cup baby spinach

- 1 cup grated mozzarella
- 1 tsp dried oregano
- 3 tbsp sliced black olives

Directions:

1. Preheat the oven to 400 F. Line a baking sheet with parchment paper. In a medium bowl, mix the almond flour, salt, psyllium powder, olive oil, and water until dough forms.

2. Spread the mixture on the pizza pan and bake in the oven until crusty, 10 minutes. When ready, remove the crust and spread the tomato sauce on top. Add the spinach, mozzarella cheese, oregano, and olives. Bake until the cheese melts, 15 minutes. Take out of the oven, slice and serve warm.

Nutrition Info:

- Per Serving: Calories: 167;Fat: 13g;Protein: 4g;Carbs: 6.7g.

Spicy Roasted Chickpeas

Servings:2
Cooking Time:40 Minutes

Ingredients:

- Chickpeas
- 1 tbsp olive oil
- 1 can chickpeas
- Salt to taste
- Seasoning Mix
- ¾ tsp cumin
- ½ tsp ground coriander
- Salt and black pepper to taste
- ¼ tsp chili powder
- ½ tsp cayenne pepper
- ¼ tsp cardamom
- ¼ tsp cinnamon
- ¼ tsp allspice

Directions:

1. Preheat oven to 400 F. In a small bowl, place all the seasoning mix ingredients and stir well to combine.

2. Place the chickpeas in a bowl and season them with olive oil and salt. Add the chickpeas to a lined baking sheet and roast them for about 25-35 minutes, turning them over once or twice while cooking until they are slightly crisp. Remove to a bowl and sprinkle them with the seasoning mix. Toss lightly to combine. Serve and enjoy!

Nutrition Info:

- Per Serving: Calories: 268;Fat: 11g;Protein: 11g;Carbs: 35g.

Speedy Granita

Servings:4
Cooking Time:10 Min + Freezing Time

Ingredients:

- ¼ cup sugar
- 1 cup fresh strawberries

- 1 cup fresh raspberries
- 1 cup chopped fresh kiwi
- 1 tsp lemon juice

Directions:

1. Bring 1 cup water to a boil in a small saucepan over high heat. Add the sugar and stir well until dissolved. Remove the pan from the heat, add the fruit and lemon juice, and cool to room temperature. Once cooled, puree the fruit in a blender until smooth. Pour the puree into a shallow glass baking dish and place in the freezer for 1 hour. Stir with a fork and freeze for 30 minutes, then repeat. Serve and enjoy!

Nutrition Info:

- Per Serving: Calories: 153;Fat: 0.2g;Protein: 1.6g;Carbs: 39g.

Cantaloupe & Watermelon Balls

Servings:4
Cooking Time:5 Min + Chilling Time

Ingredients:

- 2 cups watermelon balls
- 2 cups cantaloupe balls
- ½ cup orange juice
- ¼ cup lemon juice
- 1 tbsp orange zest

Directions:

1. Place the watermelon and cantaloupe in a bowl. In another bowl, mix the lemon juice, orange juice and zest. Pour over the fruit. Transfer to the fridge covered for 5 hours. Serve.

Nutrition Info:

- Per Serving: Calories: 71;Fat: 0g;Protein: 1.5g;Carbs: 18g.

Charred Asparagus

Servings:4
Cooking Time:25 Minutes

Ingredients:

- 2 tbsp olive oil
- 1 lb asparagus, trimmed
- 4 tbsp Grana Padano, grated
- ½ tsp garlic powder
- Salt to taste
- 2 tbsp parsley, chopped

Directions:

1. Preheat the grill to high. Season the asparagus with salt and garlic powder and coat with olive oil. Grill the asparagus for 10 minutes, turning often until lightly charred and tender. Sprinkle with cheese and parsley and serve.

Nutrition Info:

- Per Serving: Calories: 105;Fat: 8g;Protein: 4.3g;Carbs: 4.7g.

Two-cheese Stuffed Bell Peppers

Servings:6
Cooking Time:20 Min + Chilling Time
Ingredients:

- 1 ½ lb bell peppers, cored and seeded
- 1 tbsp extra-virgin olive oil
- 4 oz ricotta cheese
- 4 oz mascarpone cheese
- 1 tbsp scallions, chopped
- 1 tbsp lemon zest

Directions:

1. Preheat oven to 400 F. Coat the peppers with olive oil, put them on a baking sheet, and roast for 8 minutes. Remove and let cool. In a bowl, add the ricotta cheese, mascarpone cheese, scallions, and lemon zest. Stir to combine, then spoon mixture into a piping bag. Stuff each pepper to the top with the cheese mixture. Chill the peppers and serve.

Nutrition Info:

- Per Serving: Calories: 141;Fat: 11g;Protein: 4g;Carbs: 6g.

Turkey Pesto Pizza

Servings:4
Cooking Time:35 Minutes
Ingredients:

- Pizza Crust
- 3 tbsp olive oil
- 3 cups flour
- ¼ tsp salt
- 3 large eggs
- Topping
- ½ lb turkey ham, chopped
- 2 tbsp cashew nuts
- 1 green bell pepper, sliced
- 1 ½ cups basil pesto
- 1 cup mozzarella, grated
- 2 tbsp Parmesan cheese, grated
- 4 fresh basil leaves, chopped
- ¼ tsp red pepper flakes

Directions:

1. In a bowl, mix flour, olive oil, salt, and egg until a dough forms. Mold the dough into a ball and place it in between two full parchment papers on a flat surface. Roll it out into a circle of a ¼ -inch thickness. After, slide the pizza dough into the pizza pan and remove the parchment paper. Place the pizza pan in the oven and bake the dough for 20 minutes at 350 F. Once the pizza bread is ready, remove it from the oven, fold and seal the extra inch of dough at its edges to make a crust around it. Apply 2/3 of the pesto on it and sprinkle half of the mozzarella cheese too.

2. Toss the chopped turkey ham in the remaining pesto and spread it on top of the pizza. Sprinkle with the remaining mozzarella, bell peppers, and cashew nuts and put the pizza back in the oven to bake for 9 minutes. When it is ready, remove from the oven to cool slightly, garnish with the basil leaves and sprinkle with parmesan cheese and red pepper flakes. Slice and serve.

Nutrition Info:

- Per Serving: Calories: 684;Fat: 54g;Protein: 32g;Carbs: 22g.

Bruschetta With Tomato & Basil

Servings:4
Cooking Time:20 Minutes
Ingredients:

- 1 ciabatta loaf, halved lengthwise
- 2 tbsp olive oil
- 3 tbsp basil, chopped
- 4 tomatoes, cubed
- 1 shallot, sliced
- 2 garlic cloves, minced
- Salt and black pepper to taste
- 1 tbsp balsamic vinegar
- ½ tsp garlic powder

Directions:

1. Preheat the oven to 380 F. Line a baking sheet with parchment paper. Cut in half each half of the ciabatta loaf. Place them on the sheet and sprinkle with some olive oil. Bake for 10 minutes. Mix tomatoes, shallot, basil, garlic, salt, pepper, olive oil, vinegar, and garlic powder in a bowl and let sit for 10 minutes. Apportion the mixture among bread pieces.

Nutrition Info:

- Per Serving: Calories: 170;Fat: 5g;Protein: 5g;Carbs: 30g.

Shallot & Kale Spread

Servings:4
Cooking Time:10 Minutes
Ingredients:

- 2 shallots, chopped
- 1 lb kale, roughly chopped
- 2 tbsp mint, chopped
- ¾ cup cream cheese, soft
- Salt and black pepper to taste

Directions:

1. In a food processor, blend kale, shallots, mint, cream cheese, salt, and pepper until smooth. Serve.

Nutrition Info:

- Per Serving: Calories: 210;Fat: 12g;Protein: 6g;Carbs: 5g.

Baked Sweet Potatoes With Chickpeas

Servings:4
Cooking Time:30 Minutes
Ingredients:

- 4 sweet potatoes, halved lengthways
- 2 tbsp olive oil
- 1 tbsp butter
- 1 can chickpeas
- ¼ tsp dried thyme
- Salt and black pepper to taste
- 1 tsp paprika
- ½ tsp garlic powder
- 1 cup spinach
- 1 cup Greek-style yogurt
- 2 tsp hot sauce

Directions:

1. Preheat oven to 360 F. Drizzle the sweet potatoes with some oil. Place, cut-side down, in a lined baking tray and bake for 8-10 minutes. In a bowl, mix chickpeas with remaining olive oil, paprika, thyme, and garlic powder. Pour them onto the other end of the baking tray and roast for 20 minutes alongside the sweet potatoes, stirring the chickpeas once.

2. Melt the butter in a pan over medium heat and stir-fry the spinach and 1 tbsp of water for 3-4 minutes until the spinach wilts. Stir in the roasted chickpeas. Mix the yogurt with hot sauce in a small bowl. Top the sweet potato halves with chickpeas and spinach and serve with hot yogurt on the side.

Nutrition Info:

- Per Serving: Calories: 97;Fat: 3g;Protein: 5g;Carbs: 14g.

Country Pizza

Servings:4
Cooking Time:45 Minutes
Ingredients:

- For the crust
- 2 tbsp olive oil
- 2 cups flour
- 1 cup lukewarm water
- 1 pinch of sugar
- 1 tsp active dry yeast
- ¾ tsp salt
- For the ranch sauce
- 1 tbsp butter
- 2 garlic cloves, minced
- 1 tbsp cream cheese
- ¼ cup half and half
- 1 tbsp Ranch seasoning mix
- For the topping

- 3 bacon slices, chopped
- 2 chicken breasts
- Salt and black pepper to taste
- 1 cup grated mozzarella
- 6 fresh basil leaves

Directions:

1. Sift the flour and salt in a bowl and stir in yeast. Mix lukewarm water, olive oil, and sugar in another bowl. Add the wet mixture to the dry mixture and whisk until you obtain a soft dough. Place the dough on a lightly floured work surface and knead it thoroughly for 4-5 minutes until elastic. Transfer the dough to a greased bowl. Cover with cling film and leave to rise for 50-60 minutes in a warm place until doubled in size. Roll out the dough to a thickness of around 12 inches.

2. Preheat the oven to 400 F. Line a pizza pan with parchment paper. In a bowl, mix the sauce's ingredients butter, garlic, cream cheese, half and half, and ranch mix. Set aside. Heat a grill pan over medium heat and cook the bacon until crispy and brown, 5 minutes. Transfer to a plate and set aside.

3. Season the chicken with salt, pepper and grill in the pan on both sides until golden brown, 10 minutes. Remove to a plate, allow cooling and cut into thin slices. Spread the ranch sauce on the pizza crust, followed by the chicken and bacon, and then, mozzarella cheese and basil. Bake for 5 minutes or until the cheese melts. Slice and serve warm.

Nutrition Info:

- Per Serving: Calories: 528;Fat: 28g;Protein: 61g;Carbs: 5g.

Roasted Garlic & Spicy Lentil Dip

Servings:6
Cooking Time:40 Minutes
Ingredients:

- 1 roasted red bell pepper, chopped
- 4 tbsp olive oil
- 1 cup split red lentils
- ½ red onion
- 1 garlic bulb, top removed
- ½ tsp cumin seeds
- 1 tsp coriander seeds
- ¼ cup walnuts
- 2 tbsp tomato paste
- ½ tsp Cayenne powder
- Salt and black pepper to taste

Directions:

1. Preheat oven to 370 F. Drizzle the garlic with some olive oil and wrap it in a piece of aluminum foil. Roast for 35-40 minutes. Remove and allow to cool for a few minutes. Cover the lentils with salted water in a pot over medium heat and bring to a boil. Simmer for 15 minutes. Drain and set aside.

2. Squeeze out the garlic cloves and place them in a food processor. Add in the cooled lentils, cumin seeds, coriander seeds, roasted red bell pepper, onion, walnuts, tomato paste, Cayenne powder, remaining olive oil, salt, and black pepper. Pulse until smooth. Serve with crostiniif desire.

Nutrition Info:

- Per Serving: Calories: 234;Fat: 13g;Protein: 9g;Carbs: 21.7g.

Eggplant & Pepper Spread On Toasts

Servings:4
Cooking Time:10 Minutes
Ingredients:

- 1 red bell pepper, roasted and chopped
- 1 lb eggplants, baked, peeled and chopped
- ¾ cup olive oil
- 1 lemon, zested
- 1 red chili pepper, chopped
- 1 ½ tsp capers
- 1 garlic clove, minced
- Salt and black pepper to taste
- 1 baguette, sliced and toasted

Directions:

1. In a food processor, place the eggplants, lemon zest, red chili pepper, bell pepper, garlic, salt, and pepper. Blend while gradually adding the olive oil until smooth. Spread each baguette slice with the spread and top with capers to serve.

Nutrition Info:

- Per Serving: Calories: 364;Fat: 38g;Protein: 1.5g;Carbs: 9.3g.

Portuguese Orange Mug Cake

Servings:2
Cooking Time:12 Minutes
Ingredients:

- 2 tbsp butter, melted
- 6 tbsp flour
- 2 tbsp sugar
- ½ tsp baking powder
- ¼ tsp salt
- 1 tsp orange zest
- 1 egg
- 2 tbsp orange juice
- 2 tbsp milk
- ½ tsp orange extract
- ½ tsp vanilla extract
- Orange slices for garnish

Directions:

1. In a bowl, beat the egg, butter, orange juice, milk, orange extract, and vanilla extract. In another bowl, combine the flour, sugar, baking powder, salt, and orange zest. Pour the dry ingredients into the wet ingredients and stir to combine. Spoon the mixture into 2 mugs and microwave one at a time for 1-2 minutes. Garnish with orange slices.

Nutrition Info:

- Per Serving: Calories: 302;Fat: 17g;Protein: 6g;Carbs: 33g.

The Best Anchovy Tapenade

Servings:4
Cooking Time:10 Minutes
Ingredients:

- 1 cup roasted red peppers, chopped
- 3 tbsp olive oil
- 2 anchovy fillets, chopped
- 2 tbsp parsley, chopped
- 14 oz canned artichokes
- ¼ cup capers, drained
- 1 tbsp lemon juice
- 2 garlic cloves, minced

Directions:

1. In a food processor, blend roasted peppers, anchovies, parsley, artichokes, oil, capers, lemon juice, and garlic until a paste is formed. Serve at room temperature

Nutrition Info:

- Per Serving: Calories: 210;Fat: 6g;Protein: 5g;Carbs: 13g.

Italian Popcorn

Servings:6
Cooking Time:20 Minutes
Ingredients:

- 2 tbsp butter, melted
- 1 tbsp truffle oil
- 8 cups air-popped popcorn
- 2 tbsp packed brown sugar
- 2 tbsp Italian seasoning
- ¼ tsp sea salt

Directions:

1. Preheat oven to 350 F. Combine butter, Italian seasoning, sugar, and salt in a bowl. Pour over the popcorn and toss well to coat. Remove to a baking dish and bake for 15 minutes, stirring frequently. Drizzle with truffle oil and serve.

Nutrition Info:

- Per Serving: Calories: 80;Fat: 5g;Protein: 1.1g;Carbs: 8.4g.

Classic Tzatziki Dip

Servings:6
Cooking Time:10 Min + Chilling Time
Ingredients:
- 1 large cucumber, grated
- 1 garlic clove, minced
- 1 cup Greek yogurt
- 1 tsp chopped fresh dill
- 1 tsp chopped fresh parsley
- Salt and black pepper to taste
- ¼ cup ground walnuts

Directions:
1. In a colander over the sink, squeeze the excess liquid out of the grated cucumber. Combine the yogurt, cucumber, garlic, salt, dill, and pepper in a bowl. Keep in the fridge covered for 2 hours. Serve topped with ground walnuts and parsley.

Nutrition Info:
- Per Serving: Calories: 66;Fat: 3.8g;Protein: 5g;Carbs: 4g.

Chocolate-avocado Cream

Servings:4
Cooking Time:10 Min + Chilling Time
Ingredients:
- 2 avocados, mashed
- ¼ cup cocoa powder
- ¼ cup heavy whipping cream
- 2 tsp vanilla extract
- 2 tbsp sugar
- ½ tsp ground cinnamon
- ¼ tsp salt

Directions:
1. Blend the avocado, cocoa powder, heavy whipping cream, vanilla, sugar, cinnamon, and salt into a large bowl until smooth and creamy. Cover and refrigerate for at least 1 hour.

Nutrition Info:
- Per Serving: Calories: 230;Fat: 22g;Protein: 3g;Carbs: 10g.

Garbanzo Patties With Cilantro-yogurt Sauce

Servings:4
Cooking Time:20 Minutes
Ingredients:
- ¼ cup olive oil
- 3 garlic cloves, minced
- 1 cup canned garbanzo beans
- 2 tbsp parsley, chopped
- 1 onion, chopped
- 1 tsp ground coriander
- Salt and black pepper to taste
- ¼ tsp cayenne pepper
- ¼ tsp cumin powder
- 1 tsp lemon juice
- 3 tbsp flour
- ¼ cup Greek yogurt
- 2 tbsp chopped cilantro
- ½ tsp garlic powder

Directions:
1. In a blender, blitz garbanzo, parsley, onion, garlic, salt, pepper, ground coriander, cayenne pepper, cumin powder, and lemon juice until smooth. Remove to a bowl and mix in flour. Form 16 balls out of the mixture and flatten them into patties.
2. Warm the olive oil in a skillet over medium heat and fry patties for 10 minutes on both sides. Remove them to a paper towel–lined plate to drain the excess fat. In a bowl, mix the Greek yogurt, cilantro, garlic powder, salt, and pepper. Serve the patties with yogurt sauce.

Nutrition Info:
- Per Serving: Calories: 120;Fat: 7g;Protein: 4g;Carbs: 13g.

Baked Beet Fries With Feta Cheese

Servings:4
Cooking Time:40 Minutes
Ingredients:
- 1 cup olive oil
- 1 cup feta cheese, crumbled
- 2 beets, sliced
- Salt and black pepper to taste
- 1/3 cup balsamic vinegar

Directions:
1. Preheat the oven to 340 F. Line a baking sheet with parchment paper. Arrange beet slices, salt, pepper, vinegar, and olive oil on the sheet and toss to combine. Bake for 30 minutes. Serve topped with feta cheese.

Nutrition Info:
- Per Serving: Calories: 210;Fat: 6g;Protein: 4g;Carbs: 9g.

Greek Yogurt & Za'atar Dip On Grilled Pitta

Servings:6
Cooking Time:10 Minutes
Ingredients:
- 1/3 cup olive oil
- 2 cups Greek yogurt
- 2 tbsp toasted ground pistachios
- Salt and white pepper to taste
- 2 tbsp mint, chopped
- 3 kalamata olives, chopped
- ¼ cup za'atar seasoning

- 3 pitta breads, cut into triangles

Directions:

1. Mix the yogurt, pistachios, salt, pepper, mint, olives, za´atar spice, and olive oil in a bowl. Grill the pitta bread until golden, about 5-6 minutes. Serve with the yogurt spread.

Nutrition Info:

- Per Serving: Calories: 300;Fat: 19g;Protein: 11g;Carbs: 22g.

Vanilla Cheesecake Squares

Servings:6

Cooking Time:55 Min + Chilling Time

Ingredients:

- ½ cup butter, melted
- 1 box butter cake mix
- 3 large eggs
- 1 cup maple syrup
- 1/8 tsp cinnamon
- 1 cup cream cheese
- 1 tsp vanilla extract

Directions:

1. Preheat oven to 350 F. In a medium bowl, blend the cake mix, butter, cinnamon, and 1 egg. Then, pour the mixture into a greased baking pan. Mix together maple syrup, cream cheese, the remaining 2 eggs, and vanilla in a separate bowl and pour this gently over the first layer. Bake for 45-50 minutes. Remove and allow to cool. Cut into squares.

Nutrition Info:

- Per Serving: Calories: 160;Fat: 8g;Protein: 2g;Carbs: 20g.

Thyme Lentil Spread

Servings:6

Cooking Time:10 Minutes

Ingredients:

- 3 tbsp olive oil
- 1 garlic clove, minced
- 1 cup split red lentils, rinsed
- ½ tsp dried thyme
- 1 tbsp balsamic vinegar
- Salt and black pepper to taste

Directions:

1. Bring to a boil salted water in a pot over medium heat. Add in the lentils and cook for 15 minutes until cooked through. Drain and set aside to cool. In a food processor, place the lentils, garlic, thyme, vinegar, salt, and pepper. Gradually add olive oil while blending until smooth. Serve.

Nutrition Info:

- Per Serving: Calories: 295;Fat: 10g;Protein: 10g;Carbs: 16g.

Strawberries With Balsamic Vinegar

Servings:2

Cooking Time: 0 Minutes

Ingredients:

- 2 cups strawberries, hulled and sliced
- 2 tablespoons sugar
- 2 tablespoons balsamic vinegar

Directions:

1. Place the sliced strawberries in a bowl, sprinkle with the sugar, and drizzle lightly with the balsamic vinegar.

2. Toss to combine well and allow to sit for about 10 minutes before serving.

Nutrition Info:

- Per Serving: Calories: 92;Fat: 0.4g;Protein: 1.0g;Carbs: 21.7g.

Honeyed Pistachio Dumplings

Servings:4

Cooking Time:25 Minutes

Ingredients:

- 1 cup vegetable oil
- ½ cup warm milk
- 2 cups flour
- 2 eggs, beaten
- 1 tsp sugar
- 1 ½ oz active dry yeast
- 1 cup warm water
- ½ tsp vanilla extract
- 1 tsp cinnamon
- 1 orange, zested
- 4 tbsp honey
- 2 tbsp pistachios, chopped

Directions:

1. In a bowl, sift the flour and combine it with the cinnamon and orange zest. In another bowl, mix the sugar, yeast, and ½ cup of warm water. Leave to stand until the yeast dissolves. Stir in milk, eggs, vanilla, and flour mixture. Beat with an electric mixer until smooth. Cover the bowl with plastic wrap and let sit to rise in a warm place for at least 1 hour.

2. Pour the vegetable oil into a deep pan or wok to come halfway up the sides and heat the oil. Add some more oil if necessary. Using a teaspoon, form balls, one by one, and drop in the hot oil one after another. Fry the balls on all sides, until golden brown. Remove them with a slotted spoon to paper towels to soak the excess fat. Repeat the process until the dough is exhausted. Drizzle with honey and sprinkle with pistachios.

Nutrition Info:

- Per Serving: Calories: 890;Fat: 59g;Protein: 15g;Carbs: 78g.

Lamb Ragu Tagliatelle

Servings:4
Cooking Time:25 Minutes
Ingredients:
- 2 tbsp olive oil
- 16 oz tagliatelle
- 1 tsp paprika
- 1 tsp cumin
- Salt and black pepper to taste
- 1 lb ground lamb
- 1 cup onions, chopped
- ¼ cup parsley, chopped
- 2 garlic cloves, minced

Directions:
1. Boil the tagliatelle in a pot over medium heat for 9-11 minutes or until "al dente". Drain and set aside.
2. Warm the olive oil in a skillet over medium heat and sauté lamb, onions, and garlic until the meat is browned, about 10-15 minutes. Stir in cumin, paprika, salt, and pepper for 1-2 minutes. Spoon tagliatelle on a platter and scatter lamb over. Top with parsley and serve.

Nutrition Info:
- Per Serving: Calories: 140;Fat: 10g;Protein: 6g;Carbs: 7g.

Anchovy Stuffed Avocado Boats

Servings:4
Cooking Time:10 Minutes
Ingredients:
- 4 anchovy fillets, chopped
- 1 avocado, halved and pitted
- 2 tbsp sun-dried tomatoes, chopped
- 1 tbsp basil pesto
- 2 tbsp black olives, pitted and chopped
- Salt and black pepper to taste
- 2 tsp pine nuts, toasted
- 1 tbsp basil, chopped

Directions:
1. Toss anchovies, sun-dried tomatoes, basil pesto, olives, salt, pepper, pine nuts, and basil in a bowl. Fill each avocado half with the mixture and serve immediately.

Nutrition Info:
- Per Serving: Calories: 240;Fat: 10g;Protein: 6g;Carbs: 12g.

Parsley Lamb Arancini

Servings:4
Cooking Time:25 Minutes
Ingredients:
- 3 tbsp olive oil
- 1 lb ground lamb
- ½ tsp cumin, ground
- 1 garlic clove, minced
- Salt and black pepper to taste
- 1 cup rice
- 2 cups vegetable broth
- ¼ cup parsley, chopped
- ¼ cup shallots, chopped
- ½ tsp allspice
- 2 eggs, lightly beaten
- 1 cup breadcrumbs

Directions:
1. Cook the rice in the vegetable broth for about 15 minutes. Remove from the heat and leave to cool uncovered. In a large bowl, mix the cooled rice, ground lamb, cumin, garlic, salt, pepper, parsley, shallots, and allspice until combined. Form medium balls out of the mixture. Dip the arancini in the beaten eggs and toss in the breadcrumbs. Warm the olive oil in a skillet over medium heat and fry meatballs for 14 minutes on all sides until golden brown. Remove to paper towels to absorb excess oil. Serve warm.

Nutrition Info:
- Per Serving: Calories: 310;Fat: 10g;Protein: 7g;Carbs: 23g.

INDEX

Beet And Watercress Salad 37

Bell Pepper & Bean Salad 47

Bell Pepper & Shrimp Salad With Avocado 57

Bell Pepper, Tomato & Egg Salad 61

Bolognese Penne Bake 52

Broccoli And Carrot Pasta Salad 45

Brown Rice Pilaf With Pistachios And Raisins 45

Bruschetta With Tomato & Basil 82

Bulgur Pilaf With Kale And Tomatoes 53

C

Cannellini Bean & Chicken Cassoulet 67

Cantaloupe & Watermelon Balls 81

Caper & Squid Stew 30

Caprese Pasta With Roasted Asparagus 50

Catalan Chicken In Romesco Sauce 74

Celery And Mustard Greens 38

Chargrilled Vegetable Kebabs 40

Charred Asparagus 81

Cheese & Broccoli Quiche 57

Cheesy Fig Pizzas With Garlic Oil 22

Cheesy Smoked Salmon Crostini 24

Cherry, Apricot, And Pecan Brown Rice Bowl 45

Chicken And Pastina Soup 59

Chicken Balls With Yogurt-cucumber Sauce 71

Chicken Bruschetta Burgers 68

Chicken Gyros With Tzatziki Sauce 68

Chicken Thighs With Roasted Artichokes 72

Chickpea & Broccoli Salad 65

Chickpea Lettuce Wraps With Celery 38

Chili & Cheese Frittata 18

Chili Grilled Eggplant Rounds 80

Chili Vegetable Skillet 36

Chocolate-avocado Cream 85

Chorizo & Fire-roasted Tomato Soup 57

Citrus French Toasts 18

Classic Prawn Scampi 33

Classic Socca 16

Classic Spanish Tortilla With Tuna 13

Classic Tzatziki Dip 85

Cod Fillets In Mushroom Sauce 32

Coriander Pork Roast 75

Country Pizza 83

Cream Peach Smoothie 16

Creamy Mussel Spaghetti 55

Creamy Peach Smoothie 13

Crispy Pesto Chicken 71

Crustless Tiropita (greek Cheese Pie) 20

Cucumber & Spelt Salad With Chicken 59

Curry Apple Couscous With Leeks And Pecans 48

D

Dragon Pork Chops With Pickle Topping 70

E

Easy Alfalfa Sprout And Nut Rolls 17

Easy Blueberry And Oat Crisp 79

Easy Bulgur Tabbouleh 51

Easy Grilled Pork Chops 73

Easy Pork Stew(2) 69

Easy Simple Pesto Pasta 53

Easy Spring Salad 60

Easy Tomato Tuna Melts 32

Easy Zucchini & Egg Stuffed Tomatoes 15

Egg & Potato Salad 65

Eggplant & Pepper Spread On Toasts 84

F

Falafel Balls With Tahini Sauce 14

Fennel Beef Ribs 76

Fennel Salad With Olives & Hazelnuts 58

Fluffy Almond Flour Pancakes With Strawberries 21

Fried Eggplant Rolls 42

G

Garbanzo Patties With Cilantro-yogurt Sauce 85

Garlic And Parsley Chickpeas 50

H

I

J

Juicy Basil-tomato Scallops 25

K

Kale Chicken With Pappardelle 49

Kale-proscuitto Porridge 16

L

Lamb Ragu Tagliatelle 87

Lamb Tagine With Couscous And Almonds 74

Lemon Cioppino 28

Lemon Shrimp With Black Olives 27

Lemon-parsley Swordfish 27

Lemony Green Quinoa 52

Lemony Tuna Barley With Capers 45

Lemony Yogurt Sauce 60

Lentil And Mushroom Pasta 47

Lime Watermelon Yogurt Smoothie 16

Lime-orange Squid Meal 30

Linguine A La Carbonara 53

M

Maple Berry & Walnut Oatmeal 17

Marinated Mushrooms And Olives 63

Marrakech-style Couscous 48

Mashed Beans With Cumin 49

Mediterranean Cod Stew 33

Mediterranean Grilled Sea Bass 27

Mediterranean Tomato Hummus Soup 57

Mediterranean-style Beans And Greens 54

Milky Pork Stew 76

Minty Broccoli & Walnuts 36

Minty Lamb Risotto 55

Mixed Salad With Balsamic Honey Dressing 59

Morning Pizza Frittata 21

Moroccan Tagine With Vegetables 41

Mozzarella & Asparagus Pasta 52

Mushroom & Bell Pepper Salad 60

Mushroom & Cauliflower Roast 39

Rice & Lentil Salad With Caramelized Onions 52

Rice And Blueberry Stuffed Sweet Potatoes 50

Rice Stuffed Bell Peppers 60

Rich Chicken And Small Pasta Broth 62

Roasted Artichokes 39

Roasted Eggplant Hummus 80

Roasted Garlic & Spicy Lentil Dip 83

Roasted Pepper & Tomato Soup 63

Roasted Pork Tenderloin With Apple Sauce 71

Roasted Trout Stuffed With Veggies 25

Roasted Vegetable Medley 34

Roasted Veggies And Brown Rice Bowl 39

Root Veggie Soup 63

Rosemary Fennel In Cherry Tomato Sauce 73

Rosemary Garlic Infused Olive Oil 58

S

Salmon & Celery Egg Bake 30

Salmon & Curly Endive Salad 61

Salmon And Mushroom Hash With Pesto 31

Salmon Baked In Foil 24

Salt And Pepper Calamari And Scallops 29

Samosas In Potatoes 18

Saucy Cod With Calamari Rings 24

Saucy Turkey With Ricotta Cheese 75

Sautéed Cabbage With Parsley 44

Sautéed Ground Turkey With Brown Rice 69

Sautéed Spinach And Leeks 44

Shallot & Kale Spread 82

Shrimp And Pea Paella 33

Shrimp Quinoa Bowl With Black Olives 26

Sicilian-style Squid With Zucchini 26

Simple Green Rice 56

Simple Honey-glazed Baby Carrots 35

Simple Lentil Risotto 46

Simple Oven-baked Green Beans 37

Simple Peanut Butter And Chocolate Balls 79

Simple Salmon With Balsamic Haricots Vert 29

Simple Zoodles 37

Skillet Eggplant & Kale Frittata 13

T

V

Printed in Great Britain
by Amazon

25069742R00057